Ridiculous KNOCK-KNOCKS

CHRIS TAIT
Illustrated by Mark Zahnd

Sterling Publishing Co., Inc.

New York

For Franklyn—who makes me ridiculously happy.

Library of Congress Cataloging-in-Publication Available

Published by Sterling Publishing Company, Inc.
387 Park Avenue South, New York, N.Y. 10016
© 2001 by Chris Tait
Distributed in Canada by Sterling Publishing
C/o Canadian Manda Group, One Atlantic Avenue, Suite 105
Toronto, Ontario, Canada M6K 3E7
Distributed in Great Britain and Europe by Chris Lloyd
463 Ashley Road, Parkstone, Poole, Dorset, BH14 0AX, England
Distributed in Australia by Capricorn Link (Australia) Pty Ltd.
P.O. Box 6651, Baulkham Hills, Business Centre, NSW 2153,
Australia
Manufactured in the United States of America

Knock-Knock!
  Who's there?
Agatha!
  Agatha who?
Agatha sore tooth! It's killing me!

Knock-Knock!
  Who's there?
Albee!
  Albee who?
Albee right back, don't move!

Knock-Knock!
  Who's there?
Alfred!
  Alfred who?
Alfred duh needle if you tie the knot!

Knock-Knock!
  Who's there?
Ali!
  Ali who?
Ali wanna do is dance!

Knock-Knock!
  Who's there?
Alien Don!
  Alien Don who?
Alien Don the wet paint and ruined my shirt!

Knock-Knock!
  Who's there?
Alligator!
  Alligator who?
Alligator for her birthday was a card!

Knock-Knock!
  Who's there?
Alvin!
  Alvin who?
Alvin a nice time on your porch, since you ask!

Knock-Knock!
  Who's there?
Amaso!
  Amaso who?
Amaso sorry you don't remember me!

Knock-Knock!
  Who's there?
Amy!
  Amy who?
Amy 'fraid this is the wrong house! I don't know
you either.

Knock-Knock!
  Who's there?
Amsterdam!
  Amsterdam who?
Amsterdam hungry I could eat a horse!

Knock-Knock!
  Who's there?
Andy!
  Andy who?
Andy body home?

Knock-Knock!
  Who's there?
Anita!
  Anita who?
Anita another knock-knock
joke like I need a hole in
the head!

Knock-Knock!
  Who's there?
Annie!
  Annie who?
Annie thing I can do for you today?

Knock-Knock!
  Who's there?
Answer!
  Answer who?
Answer all over your porch! It's a mess out here!

Knock-Knock!
  Who's there?
Apple!
  Apple who?
Apple on the door, but nothing happens!

Knock-Knock!
  Who's there?
Arizona!
  Arizona who?
Arizona so many
times I can knock!

Knock-Knock!
Who's there?
Arnie!
Arnie who?
Arnie ya even gonna open the door?

Knock-Knock!
Who's there?
Arnold!
Arnold who?
Arnold friend from far away!

Knock-Knock!
Who's there?
Arthur!
Arthur who?
Arthur any other kind of jokes
you know?

Knock-Knock!
Who's there?
Asia!
Asia who?
Asia matter of fact, I
don't remember!

Knock-Knock!
Who's there?
Astronaut!
Astronaut who?
Astronaut here, come back later!

Knock-Knock!
   Who's there?
Avery!
   Avery who?
Avery time I come to your house, we go through this!

Knock-Knock!
   Who's there?
Axel!
   Axel who?
Axel nicely and I might tell ya!

Knock-Knock!
  Who's there?
Bacon!
  Bacon who?
Bacon from the heat. It's sweltering out here!

Knock-Knock!
  Who's there?
Baloney!
  Baloney who?
Baloney chase you if you're a matador!

Knock-Knock!
  Who's there?
Bar-B-Q!
  Bar-B-Q who?
Bar-B-Q-t, but I think you're even cuter!

Knock-Knock!
  Who's there?
Barry!
  Barry who?
Barry happy to meet you!

Knock-Knock!
  Who's there?
Bat!
  Bat who?
Bat you can't guess!

Knock-Knock!
  Who's there?
Beaver E.!
  Beaver E. who?
Beaver E. quiet and nobody will find us!

Knock-Knock!
  Who's there?
Becka!
  Becka who?
Becka the bus is the best place to sit!

Knock-Knock!
  Who's there?
Begonia!
  Begonia who?
Begonia bother me!

Knock-Knock!
  Who's there?
Bella!
  Bella who?
Bella bottoms — they're back in style!

Knock-Knock!
  Who's there?
Bellows!
  Bellows who?
Bellows me five bucks and I've come to collect!

Knock-Knock!
  Who's there?
Ben!
  Ben who?
Ben a long time since I've seen you!

Knock-Knock!
  Who's there?
Benny!
  Benny who?
Benny thing happening?

Knock-Knock!
Who's there?
Beth!
Beth who?
Beth time for you, stinky!
Peee-uw!

Knock-Knock!
Who's there?
Betty!
Betty who?
Betty doesn't even know his own name!

Knock-Knock!
Who's there?
Bingo!
Bingo who?
Bingo-ing to this school long?

Knock-Knock!
Who's there?
Bison!
Bison who?
Bison girl scout cookies?

Knock-Knock!
Who's there?
Boo!
Boo who?
Aw, cheer up, it's not
that bad!

12

Knock-Knock!
  Who's there?
Boris!
  Boris who?
Boris with another knock-knock joke!

Knock-Knock!
  Who's there?
Bossy!
  Bossy who?
Bossy just fired me!

Knock-Knock!
  Who's there?
Buckle!
  Buckle who?
Buckle get you a soda pop, but not much else!

Knock-Knock!
  Who's there?
Bullet!
  Bullet who?
Bullet all the hay and now he's hungry!

Knock-Knock!
  Who's there?
Bunny!
  Bunny who?
Bunny thing is, I know where the Easter eggs are!

Knock-Knock!
   Who's there?
Burton!
   Burton who?
Burton me are going fishing, want to come?

Knock-Knock!
   Who's there?
Butcher!
   Butcher who?
Butcher shoulder to the door and push!

Knock-Knock!
   Who's there?
Butter!
   Butter who?
Butter stay
inside — it looks
like rain!

C

Knock-Knock!
  Who's there?
Caesar!
  Caesar who?
Caesar before she fills her squirt gun!

Knock-Knock!
  Who's there?
Candice!
  Candice who?
Candice be love?

Knock-Knock!
  Who's there?
Cannelloni!
  Cannelloni who?
Cannelloni five bucks till next week?

Knock-Knock!
  Who's there?
Canoe!
  Canoe who?
Canoe please open the door?

Knock-Knock!
  Who's there?
Cantelope!
  Cantelope who?
Cantelope, my parents have already planned the
wedding!

Knock-Knock!
  Who's there?
Canter!
  Canter who?
Canter brother come out and play?

Knock-Knock!
  Who's there?
Cargo!
  Cargo who?
Cargo really fast when
you step on the gas!

Knock-Knock!
  Who's there?
Carrie!
  Carrie who?
Carrie this for me, will you, my back's killing me!

Knock-Knock!
  Who's there?
Carrier!
  Carrier who?
Carrier own books, lazybones!

Knock-Knock!
  Who's there?
Carrot!
  Carrot who?
Carrot all for me?

Knock-Knock!
  Who's there?
Cartoon!
  Cartoon who?
Cartoon up just fine, she
purrs like a kitten!

Knock-Knock!
  Who's there?
Catgut!
  Catgut who?
Catgut yer tongue?

Knock-Knock!
  Who's there?
Catsup!
  Catsup who?
Catsup on the roof — want me to go get him?

Knock-Knock!
  Who's there?
Cauliflower!
  Cauliflower who?
Cauliflower by any other name and it's still a daisy!

Will you be my valentine?

Knock-Knock!
  Who's there?
Cecil!
  Cecil who?
Cecil seashells by
the seashore!

Knock-Knock!
  Who's there?
Cello!
  Cello who?
Cello dere, dahling, how ah ya?

Knock-Knock!
  Who's there?
Chair!
  Chair who?
Chair you go again, asking silly questions!

Knock-Knock!
  Who's there?
Checkmate!
  Checkmate who?
Checkmate bounce if you don't put money in the
bank!

Knock-Knock!
 Who's there?
Chester!
 Chester who?
Chester voice from the past!

Knock-Knock!
 Who's there?
Chesterton!
 Chesterton who?
Chesterton of fun!

Knock-Knock!
 Who's there?
Chestnut!
 Chestnut who?
Chestnut easy to open, we need a key!

Knock-Knock!
 Who's there?
Claire!
 Claire who?
Claire the way, I'm coming through!

Knock-Knock!
 Who's there?
Clothesline!
 Clothesline who?
Clothesline all over the floor end up wrinkled!

Knock-Knock!
  Who's there?
Coffin!
  Coffin who?
Coffin that bad means you got a cold!

Knock-Knock!
  Who's there?
Cole!
  Cole who?
Cole me later, I gotta go!

Knock-Knock!
  Who's there?
Colleen!
  Colleen who?
Colleen all cars, Colleen all cars! We have a knock-knock joke in progress!

Knock-Knock!
  Who's there?
Cook!
  Cook who?
You're the one who's cuckoo!

Knock-Knock!
  Who's there?
Cookie!
  Cookie who?
Cookie quit and now I have to make all the food myself!

Knock-Knock!
  Who's there?
Comb!
  Comb who?
Comb on down and I'll tell you!

Knock-Knock!
  Who's there?
Conover.
  Conover who?
Conover remember the punch line!

Knock-Knock!
  Who's there?
Copperfield!
  Copperfield who?
Copperfield bad so I came instead!

That's "whom" not "who".

Knock-Knock!
  Who's there?
Cows go!
    Cows go who?
No, they don't — cows go moo!

Knock-Knock!
  Who's there?
Crewcut!
  Crewcut who?
Crewcut out and I'm the only one left!

21

Knock-Knock!
  Who's there?
Cupid!
  Cupid who?
Cupid quiet in there!

Knock-Knock!
  Who's there?
Cumin!
  Cumin who?
Cumin side, it's freezing out there!

Knock-Knock!
  Who's there?
Cymbals!
  Cymbals who?
Cymbals have horns and
others don't!

D

Knock-Knock!
Who's there?
Daisy!
   Daisy who?
Daisy like his new school?

Knock-Knock!
   Who's there?
Dancer!
   Dancer who?
Dancer is simple! It's me!

Knock-Knock!
   Who's there?
   Daniella!
      Daniella who?
Daniella so loud, I
can hear you just
fine!

23

Knock-Knock!
 Who's there?
Darren!
 Darren who?
Darren you to read through to the last page of this
knock-knock book!

Knock-Knock!
 Who's there?
Darryl!
 Darryl who?
Darryl never be another girl like you!

Knock-Knock!
 Who's there?
Deena!
 Deena who?
Deena catch a single fish.

Knock-Knock!
　Who's there?
Digit!
　Digit who?
Digit least ask her to come with us?

Knock-Knock!
　Who's there?
Dion!
　Dion who?
Dion to play football, let's go!

Knock-Knock!
　Who's there?
Dinosaur!
　Dinosaur who?
Dinosaur, she fell
down playing tennis!

Knock-
Knock!
　Who's
　　there?
Disguise!
　Disguise who?
Disguise killing me with these knock-knock jokes!

Knock-Knock!
  Who's there?
Dish wash!
  Dish wash who?
Dish wash my house when I was a little kid!

Knock-Knock!
  Who's there?
Distress!
  Distress who?
Distress is better than that dress!

Knock Knock!
  Who's there?
Don!
  Don who?
Don tell me you don't remember me!

Knock-Knock!
  Who's there?
Don Juan!
  Don Juan who?
Don Juan to go to school today, let's go to the zoo!

Knock-Knock!
  Who's there?
Doughnut!
  Doughnut who?
Doughnut make me reveal my true identity! I'm
under cover!

Knock-Knock!
  Who's there?
Dougy!
  Dougy who?
Dougy hole in your lawn by accident! Sorry.

Knock-Knock!
  Who's there?
Dumbbell!
  Dumbbell who?
Dumbbell doesn't work, so I had to knock!

Knock-Knock!
  Who's there?
Dunfield!
  Dunfield who?
Dunfield good when I woke up this morning!

Knock-Knock!
　Who's there?
Earlier!
　Earlier who?
Earlier fly is undone!

Knock-Knock!
　Who's there?
Eddy!
　Eddy who?
Eddy idea how I can get rid
ub dis cold?

Knock-Knock!
　Who's there?
Eggs!
　Eggs who?
Eggs-actly what I was going to ask you!

Knock-Knock!
  Who's there?
Emma!
  Emma who?
Emma too early for lunch?

Knock-Knock!
  Who's there?
Emma Dunne!
  Emma Dunne who?
Emma Dunne talking to you? I've got better things
to do!

Knock-Knock!
  Who's there?
Emmanuelle!
  Emmanuelle who?
Emmanuelle is what I need to figure out this
intercom!

Knock-Knock!
  Who's there?
Epstein!
  Epstein who?
Epstein some crazy people, but you take the cake!

Knock-Knock!
  Who's there?
Eva!
  Eva who?
Eva going to answer the door?

Knock-Knock!
 Who's there?
Evans!
 Evans who?
Evans about to open up with rain — let me in!

Knock-Knock!
 Who's there?
Everest!
 Everest who?
Everest your eyes during class? Teacher thinks
you're sleeping.

Knock-Knock!
 Who's there?
Everlast!
 Everlast who?
Everlast one of you better come out here!

Knock-Knock!
 Who's there?
Eyeball!
 Eyeball who?
Eyeball my eyes out every time you go!

Knock-Knock!
  Who's there?
Fajita!
  Fajita who?
Fajita another burrito, I'm gonna be sick!

Knock-Knock!
  Who's there?
Falafel!
  Falafel who?
Falafel my skateboard and landed on my knee!

Knock-Knock!
  Who's there?
Fatso!
  Fatso who?
Fatso funny about all these knock-knock jokes?

Knock-Knock!
  Who's there?
Feline!
  Feline who?
Feline fine, how about you?

Knock-Knock!
  Who's there?
Felix!
  Felix who?
Felix me again, I'm not gonna pet your dog
anymore!

Knock-Knock!
  Who's there?
Ferdinand!
  Ferdinand who?
Ferdinand beats two in the bush!

Knock-Knock!
  Who's there?
Ferris!
  Ferris who?
Ferris fair, you win!

Knock-Knock!
  Who's there?
Fiddle!
  Fiddle who?
Fiddle make you happy, I'll tell you!

Knock-Knock!
  Who's there?
Fido!
  Fido who?
Fi don't come inside, I'm gonna freeze!

Knock-Knock!
  Who's there?
Fish!
  Fish who?
Fish-us temper your dog's got! He should be on a
leash!

Knock-Knock!
  Who's there?
Fission!
  Fission who?
Fission a bowl are safe
  from the cat!

Knock-Knock!
Who's there?
Fizzle!
Fizzle who?
Fizzle make ya burp!

Knock-Knock!
Who's there?
Fletcher!
Fletcher who?
Fletcher door open just a crack, I'll slip this
pizza inside!

Knock-Knock!
Who's there?
Flounder!
Flounder who?
Flounder key on the lawn — ya want it back?

Knock-Knock!
Who's there?
Fossil!
Fossil who?
Fossil last time, open the door!

Knock-Knock!
Who's there?
Francis!
Francis who?
Francis between Spain and Germany.

Knock-Knock!
  Who's there?
Frankie!
  Frankie who?
Frankie my dear, I don't give a darn!

Knock-Knock!
  Who's there?
Freda!
  Freda who?
Freda make knock-knock jokes all day long!

Knock-Knock!
  Who's there?
Freddie!
  Freddie who?
Freddie cat, why don't you come
out here and find out!

Knock-Knock!
  Who's there?
Fredo!
  Fredo who?
Fredo the dark, turn on the
porch light!

Knock-Knock!
  Who's there?
Fred N. Green!
  Fred N. Green who?
Fred N. Green are my favorite colors!

Knock-Knock!
  Who's there?
Furlong!
  Furlong who?
Furlong time I wanted to come by and say hi!

Knock-Knock!
  Who's there?
Fuschia!
  Fuschia who?
Fuschia ever call me, I'm going to be out!

Knock-Knock!
  Who's there?
Fuzzy!
  Fuzzy who?
Fuzzy sake of old times, open the door!

Knock-Knock!
  Who's there?
Gabe!
  Gabe who?
Gabe it my best shot and that's all I can do!

Knock-Knock!
  Who's there?
George!
  George who?
George-us lady, give me a kiss!

Knock-Knock!
  Who's there?
Gino!
  Gino who?
Gino who it is, I'm
your twin brother!

Knock-Knock!
 Who's there?
Giovanni!
 Giovanni who?
Giovanni go to the park with me?

Knock-Knock!
 Who's there?
Gladys!
 Gladys who?
Gladys finally summer vacation, aren't you?

Knock-Knock!
 Who's there?
Gladiola!
 Gladiola who?
Gladiola door open for me!

Knock-Knock!
 Who's there?
Gopher!
 Gopher who?
Gopher crying out loud,
stop asking!

Knock-Knock!
 Who's there?
Gorilla!
 Gorilla who?
Gorilla cheese is good with ketchup!

Knock-Knock!
  Who's there?
Grape!
  Grape who?
Grape game the other day, you're still the champ!

Knock-Knock!
  Who's there?
Greta!
  Greta who?
Greta phone and then I can stop knocking!

Knock-Knock!
  Who's there?
Guitar!
  Guitar who?
Guitar gloves and let's make a snowman!

Knock-Knock!
  Who's there?
Gunga din.
  Gunga din who?
I gunga din! That's why I'm knock-
ing on the door, goofy!

Knock-Knock!
  Who's there?
Gustavo!
  Gustavo who?
Gustavo very good idea!

H

Knock-Knock!
 Who's there?
Hairdo!
 Hairdo who?
Hairdo some crazy stuff,
lend me your comb!

Knock-Knock!
 Who's there?
Hansel!
 Hansel who?
Hansel freeze right off if
you don't let me in!

Knock-Knock!
 Who's there?
Hardy!
 Hardy who?
Hardy recognized you without
your glasses!

40

Knock-Knock!
  Who's there?
Hayden!
  Hayden who?
Hayden won't do any good — I can see you through
the mail slot!

Knock-Knock!
  Who's there?
Heavy!
  Heavy who?
Heavy ever been to
sea, Billy?

Knock-Knock!
  Who's there?
Heidi!
  Heidi who?
Heidi claire,
something
smells delicious!

Knock-Knock!
  Who's there?
Heifer!
  Heifer who?
Heifer heard so many knock-knock jokes?

Knock-Knock!
  Who's there?
Hi!
  Hi who?
Hi who, hi who, it's off to work we go!

Knock-Knock!
  Who's there?
Hockey!
  Hockey who?
Hockey doesn't work, so I had to knock!

Knock-Knock!
  Who's there?
Hole!
  Hole who?
Hole-he cow, Batman, time to head back to the cave!

Knock-Knock!
  Who's there?
Homer!
  Homer who?
Homer 'gain after a long day of school. Time for fun!

Knock-Knock!
  Who's there?
House!
  House who?
House about you let me come inside!

Knock-Knock!
 Who's there?
Howell!
 Howell who?
Howell you ever make friends if you stay locked up
like that?

Knock-Knock!
 Who's there?
Hugh!
 Hugh who?
Yes, can I help you?

Knock-Knock!
 Who's there?
Hugo!
 Hugo who?
Hugo on and on about these knock-knock jokes!

Knock-Knock!
 Who's there?
Hutch!
 Hutch who?
You sound like
you're coming
down with
something!

Knock-Knock!
  Who's there?
Icy!
  Icy who?
Icy you in there, let me in!

Knock-Knock!
  Who's there?
Ida!
  Ida who?
Ida brought my home-
work if my dog hadn't
eaten it!

Knock-Knock!
  Who's there?
Iguana!
  Iguana who?
Iguana sell you these great magazines!

Knock-Knock!
  Who's there?
India!
  India who?
India afternoon, I'm going to the dentist!

Knock-Knock!
  Who's there?
Innuendo!
  Innuendo who?
Innuendo the dinner you get dessert.

Knock-Knock!
  Who's there?
Interrupting cow!
  Interrupting (*say* "Moooooooooooo!" *as the other person is saying* "Interrupting Cow who?") cow who?

Knock-Knock!
  Who's there!
Irish!
  Irish who?
Irish you'd take me away from all this!

Knock-Knock!
  Who's there?
Isabella!
  Isabella who?
Isabella broken or what? I've been ringing forever!

Knock-Knock!
  Who's there?
Isaiah!
  Isaiah who?
Isaiah nothing else until
you let me in!

Knock-Knock!
  Who's there?
Island!
  Island who?
Island on your doorstep
and you don't let me in—
just my luck!

Knock-Knock!
  Who's there?
Issue!
  Issue who?
Issue blind? It's me!

Knock-Knock!
  Who's there?
Ivana!
  Ivana who?
Ivana go to the movie, you vanna buy me a ticket?

Knock-Knock!
  Who's there?
Jason!
  Jason who?
Jason your brother will only get you in trouble!

Knock-Knock!
  Who's there?
Jerry.
  Jerry who?
Jerry funny, you know darn well who it is!

Knock-Knock!
  Who's there?
Jess!
  Jess who?
Hey, that's my line!

Knock-Knock!
  Who's there?
Jilly!
  Jilly who?
Jilly out here, but I bet it's warm in there!

47

Knock-Knock!
  Who's there?
Jimmy!
  Jimmy who?
Jimmy back my book, you
thief!

Knock-Knock!
  Who's there?
Jiminy!
  Jiminy who?
Jiminy were at the park playing baseball.

Knock-Knock!
  Who's there?
Jo!
  Jo who?
Jo, team, Jo!

Knock-Knock!
  Who's there?
Joanna!
  Joanna who?
Joanna big kiss or what?

Knock-Knock!
  Who's there?
Joey!
  Joey who?
Joey to the world! It's Christmas!

Knock-Knock!
  Who's there?
Juan!
  Juan who?
Juan to go for a pizza?

Knock-Knock!
  Who's there?
Juanita!
  Juanita who?
Juanita sandwich with me?

Knock-Knock!
  Who's there?
Juliet.
  Juliet who?
Juliet all the pizza and there ain't none left
for me, Pa!

Knock-Knock!
  Who's there?
Julius!
  Julius who?
Julius just jealous
that you know all the
good jokes!

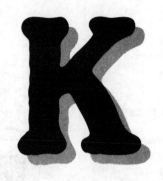

Knock-Knock!
  Who's there?
Kansas!
  Kansas who?
Kansas what tuna come in, silly!

Knock-Knock!
  Who's there?
Kenneth!
  Kenneth who?
Kenneth little kids come inthide?

Knock-Knock!
  Who's there?
Kenny!
  Kenny who?
Kenny let me in or what?

Knock-Knock!
  Who's there?
Kenya.
  Kenya who?
Kenya fix the doorbell — I've been knocking for
hours!

Knock-Knock!
  Who's there?
Kerry!
  Kerry who?
Kerry me upstairs, would you? I'm
pooped!

Knock-Knock!
  Who's there?
Ketchup!
  Ketchup who?
Ketchup on your
homework!

Knock-Knock!
Who's there?
Kitten!
Kitten who?
Kitten the park hit me with a frisbee!

Knock-Knock!
Who's there?
Klaus!
Klaus who?
Klaus the window, I can hear your television all the way down the street!

Knock-Knock!
Who's there?
Kumquat!
Kumquat who?
Kumquat may, we'll always be friends!

Knock-Knock!
  Who's there?
L.A.!
  L.A. who?
L.A. down to take a nap and slept right
through dinner!

Knock-Knock!
  Who's there?
Lego!
  Lego who?
Lego of me and I'll tell you!

Knock-Knock!
  Who's there?
Leif!
  Leif who?
Leif me alone with all
your silly questions!

Knock-Knock!
  Who's there?
Lena!
  Lena who?
Lena little closer and maybe I'll tell you!

Knock-Knock!
  Who's there?
Lettuce!
  Lettuce who?
Lettuce in or we'll huff and we'll puff and we'll blow
the house down!

Knock-Knock!
  Who's there?
Lion!
  Lion who?
Lion down on the job will get you fired!

Knock-Knock!
  Who's there?
Lisa!
  Lisa who?
Lisa you can do is let me in! It's
pouring rain!

Knock-Knock!
  Who's there?
Little old lady!
  Little old lady who?
Do you sing opera too?

Knock-Knock!
Who's there?
Liza!
Liza who?
Liza only gonna get you into trouble, buster!

Knock-Knock!
Who's there?
Lotta!
Lotta who?
Lotta knock-knocks for such a little book!

Knock-Knock!
Who's there?
Lucille!
Lucille who?
Lucille me out here — just let me in!

Knock-Knock!
Who's there?
Luncheon!
Luncheon who?
Luncheon candy and snacks and you'll get sick!

M

Knock-Knock!
  Who's there?
Mabel!
  Mabel who?
Mabel syrup is great
on waffles!

Knock-Knock!
  Who's there?
Manny!
  Manny who?
Manny people

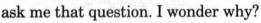

ask me that question. I wonder why?

Knock-Knock!
  Who's there?
Maria!
  Maria who?
Maria me, I love you!

Knock-Knock!
Who's there?
Maple!
Maple who?
Maple the door off
the hinges if you
don't let me in!

Don't make me pull that thing down!

Knock-Knock!
Who's there?
Markus!
Markus who?
Markus down for
two tickets, we're
going to the show!

Knock-Knock!
Who's there?
Marshall!
Marshall who?
Marshall get you covered in mud!

Knock-Knock!
Who's there?
Max!
Max who?
Max no difference how long it takes — I've got all
day!

Knock-Knock!
  Who's there?
Maya!
  Maya who?
Maya foot seems to be caught in your door!

Knock-Knock!
  Who's there?
Matthew!
  Matthew who?
Matthew need help with. Science you might be
better at!

Knock-Knock!
  Who's there?
Mercedes!
  Mercedes who?
Mercedes your best friend.

Knock-Knock!
  Who's there?
Meter!
  Meter who?
Meter at the train station at 7 o'clock sharp!

Knock-Knock!
  Who's there?
Mice!
  Mice who?
Mice to make your acquaintance!

Knock-Knock!
  Who's there?
Micro!
  Micro who?
Micro is missing — is your crow around?

REWARD!

Have you seen this crow?
Answers to the name "Spot"
Call 555-CROW

Knock-Knock!
  Who's there?
Mistake!
  Mistake who?
Mistake aspirin if you have a headache!

Knock-Knock!
  Who's there?
Mister!
  Mister who?
Mister last joke, get her to tell it again!

Knock-Knock!
  Who's there?
Mission!
  Mission who?
Mission you is making me sad, come home!

Knock-Knock!
  Who's there?
Modem!
  Modem who?
Modem lawns, the grass is getting long!

Knock-Knock!
  Who's there?
Morris!
  Morris who?
Morris code didn't work, so I had to come tell ya in
person!

Knock-Knock!
  Who's there?
Morrie!
  Morrie who?
Morrie tries to kiss me the more I run away!

Knock-Knock!
  Who's there?
Moscow!
  Moscow who?
Moscow moos but Pa's is very quiet!

Knock-Knock!
  Who's there?
Moustache!
  Moustache who?
Moustache you a question, you ready?

Knock-Knock!
  Who's there?
Mustard!
  Mustard who?
Mustard heard this one before!

N

Knock-Knock!
   Who's there?
Noah!
   Noah who?
Noah don't recognize
your voice either!

Knock-Knock!
   Who's there?
Nunio!
   Nunio who?
Nunio wanna open the door?

Knock-Knock!
  Who's there?
Obi wan!
  Obi wan who?
Obi wan of the good guys and let me in!

Knock-Knock!
  Who's there?
Oil change!
  Oil change who?
Oil change my clothes
and come back later!

Knock-Knock!
  Who's there?
Olive!
  Olive who?
Olive the times I've been to your house and you still
don't know me?

Knock-Knock!
    Who's there?
Oliver!
    Oliver who?
Oliver clothes are getting soaked, it's pouring out here!

Knock-Knock!
    Who's there?
Ollie!
    Ollie who?
Ollie want is to come inside.

Knock-Knock!
    Who's there?
Ooze!
    Ooze who?
Ooze the boss around here anyway?

Knock-Knock!
    Who's there?
Orange!
    Orange who?
Orange you gonna let me in?

Knock-Knock!
    Who's there?
Orange juice!
    Orange juice who?
Orange juice the guy I just talked to?

Knock-Knock!
  Who's there?
Otis!
  Otis who?
Otis a lie — say 'tis a lie!

Knock-Knock!
  Who's there?
Otto!
  Otto who?
Otto be asleep by now!

Knock-Knock!
  Who's there?
Owl!
  Owl who?
Owl call ya later!

Knock-Knock!
  Who's there?
Paris!
  Paris who?
Paris good but apple is better!

Knock-Knock!
  Who's there?
Pasta!
  Pasta who?
Pasta gravy please!

Knock-Knock!
  Who's there?
Pencil!
  Pencil who?
Pencil keep your legs warm!

Knock-Knock!
Who's there?
Pecan!
Pecan who?
Pecan the closet, there's a surprise for you!

Knock-Knock!
Who's there?
Pepper!
Pepper who?
Pepper up for the cheerleading rally!

Knock-Knock!
Who's there?
Pepperoni!
Pepperoni who?
Pepperoni makes me sneeze!

Knock-Knock!
Who's there?
Personal!
Personal who?
Personal catch their death of cold out here!

Knock-Knock!
Who's there?
Petunia!
Petunia who?
Petunia and me, there's only a door!

Knock-Knock!
  Who's there?
Philip!
  Philip who?
Philip my gas tank, will you?

Knock-Knock!
  Who's there?
Pickle!
  Pickle who?
Pickle little flower and give it to your mother!

Knock-Knock!
  Who's there?
Pierre!
  Pierre who?
Pierre at five o'clock and you'll find out!

Knock-Knock!
  Who's there?
Pigment!
  Pigment who?
Pigment a lot to me,
have you seen him?

Knock-Knock!
  Who's there?
Piña!
  Piña who?
Piña long time since I've seen you!

Knock-Knock!
  Who's there?
Pinafore.
  Pinafore who?
Pinafore your thoughts!

Knock-Knock!
  Who's there?
Pizza!
  Pizza who?
Pizza my coat is caught in the door!

Knock-Knock!
  Who's there?
Plane!
  Plane who?
Plane dumb won't help you now!

Knock-Knock!
  Who's there?
Poker!
  Poker who?
Poker and she'll get real mad!

Knock-Knock!
  Who's there?
Police!
  Police who?
Police let me in, it's cold out here!

Knock-Knock!
  Who's there?
Porpoise!
  Porpoise who?
Porpoise of my visit is an unpaid bill!

Knock-Knock!
  Who's there?
Puck!
  Puck who?
Puck-er up, I'm gonna kiss you!

Knock-Knock!
  Who's there?
Pumpkin!
  Pumpkin who?
Pumpkin get ya water!

Knock-Knock!
  Who's there?
Pylon!
  Pylon who?
Pylon the knock-knocks, I love 'em!

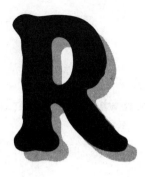

R

Knock-Knock!
  Who's there?
Rabbit!
  Rabbit who?
Rabbit around your head
like a turban!

Knock-Knock!
  Who's there?
Rain!
  Rain who?
Rain dear, you remember
me, the one with the
shiny nose?

Knock-Knock!
  Who's there?
Ray!
  Ray who?
Ray-member me?

Knock-Knock!
Who's there?
Raymond!
Raymond who?
Raymond me again what I'm doing here!

Knock-Knock!
Who's there?
Ringo!
Ringo who?
Ringo round the rosie, pocket full of posie!

Knock-Knock!
Who's there?
Riot!
Riot who?
Riot on time, here I am!

Knock-Knock!
Who's there?
Robin!
Robin who?
Robin the bank will
get you in jail!

Knock-Knock!
Who's there?
Rockies!
Rockies who?
Rockies my favorite kind of music!

Knock-Knock!
Who's there?
Romeo.
Romeo who?
Romeo-ver to the other side of the river, would ya?

Knock-Knock!
Who's there?
Ron!
Ron who?
Ron house! They all look the same!

Knock-Knock!
Who's there?
Rufus!
Rufus who?
Rufus falling in!

Knock-Knock!
Who's there?
Russell.
Russell who?
Russell me up some grub and I'll tell ya.

Knock-Knock!
　Who's there?
Salami!
　Salami who?
Salami in already!

Somebody order a salami on rye?

Knock-Knock!
　Who's there?
Salmon!
　Salmon who?
Salmon chanted evening,
you may meet a stranger!

Knock-Knock!
　Who's there?
Samson!
　Samson who?
Samson you turned out to be! You don't recognize
your own father!

Knock-Knock!
   Who's there?
Sammy!
   Sammy who?
Sammy better directions and I'll get here faster!

Knock-Knock!
   Who's there?
Sandy!
   Sandy who?
Sandy locksmith to get this door open!

Knock-Knock!
   Who's there?
San Francisco!
   San Francisco who?
San Francisco to the store — and tell him to buy
some bread!

Knock-Knock!
   Who's there?
Santa!
   Santa who?
Santa letter, but you never replied!

Knock-Knock!
   Who's there?
Sara!
   Sara who?
Sara-nother time I should come back?

Knock-Knock!
Who's there?
Sarah!
Sarah who?
Sarah reason you're not letting me in?

Knock-Knock!
Who's there?
Scotland!
Scotland who?
Scotland on his head, we have to take him to the hospital!

Knock-Knock!
Who's there?
Senior!
Senior who?
Senior so nosey, I'm not going to tell you who it is!

Knock-Knock!
Who's there?
Sesame!
Sesame who?
Sesame out here, now let me in!

Knock-Knock!
Who's there?
Sheep!
Sheep who?
Sheep-ritty, don't you think?

Knock-Knock!
　Who's there?
Sheila!
　Sheila who?
Sheila be mad if I don't deliver these flowers!

Knock-Knock!
　Who's there?
Shirley!
　Shirley who?
Shirley you must be joking!

Knock-Knock!
　Who's there?
Shoe!
　Shoe who?
Shoe, kid, ya bother me!

Knock-Knock!
　Who's there?
Shower!
　Shower who?
Shower you care and send flowers!

Knock-Knock!
　Who's there?
Sinker!
　Sinker who?
Sinker swim, it's up to you!

Knock-Knock!
  Who's there?
Simmy!
  Simmy who?
Simmy a get-well card!

Knock-Knock!
  Who's there?
Simon!
  Simon who?
Simon the other side of the door—if you opened it,
you'd know!

Knock-Knock!
  Who's there?
Simon!
  Simon who?
Simon the dotted line and all your troubles will be
over!

Knock-Knock!
  Who's there?
Snow!
  Snow who?
Snow way I'm
waiting out here
— it's freezing!

Knock-Knock!
  Who's there?
Soda!
  Soda who?
Soda sweater, it's full of holes!

Knock-Knock!
  Who's there?
Soldier!
  Soldier who?
Soldier comics yet?

Knock-Knock!
  Who's there?
Sonata!
  Sonata who?
Sonata-s bad as everybody says!

Knock-Knock!
  Who's there?
Soup!
  Soup who?
Soup-erman to the rescue!

Knock-Knock!
  Who's there?
Spain!
  Spain who?
Spain in the butt!

Knock-Knock!
  Who's there?
Sparkle!
  Sparkle who?
Sparkle start a fire if you're not careful!

Knock-Knock!
  Who's there?
Sparrow!
  Sparrow who?
Sparrow little
change, pal?

Knock-Knock!
  Who's there?
Stubborn!
  Stubborn who?
Stubborn your toe sure hurts! Ow!

Knock-Knock!
  Who's there?
Stork!
  Stork who?
Stork up on supplies — I'm staying a while!

Knock-Knock!
  Who's there?
Sunday!
  Sunday who?
Sunday in the future we'll meet in person!

80

Knock-Knock!
  Who's there?
Stan!
  Stan who?
Stan back — I'm breaking the
door down!

Knock-Knock!
  Who's there?
Sturdy!
  Sturdy who?
Sturdy pot, de soup is
burning!

Knock-Knock!
  Who's there?
Stink heap!
  Stink heap who?
EW!

Knock-Knock!
  Who's there?
Sweden!
  Sweden who?
Sweden sour chicken!

T

Knock-Knock!
 Who's there?
Tailor!
 Tailor who?
Tailor head, your choice!

Knock-Knock!
 Who's there?
Termite!
 Termite who?
Termite be something
wrong with your glasses!

Knock-Knock!
 Who's there?
Tex!
 Tex who?
Tex one to know one!

Knock-Knock!
  Who's there?
Thistle!
  Thistle who?
Thistle be the last time I visit you! Sheesh!

Knock-Knock!
  Who's there?
Tina!
  Tina who?
Tina little bug just bit me right on the nose!

Knock-Knock!
  Who's there?
Tuna!
  Tuna who?
Tuna piano and it sounds better!

Knock-Knock!
  Who's there?
Turnip!
  Turnip who?
Turnip the sound, I can't hear
the music!

Knock-Knock!
  Who's there?
Tyrone!
  Tyrone who?
Tyrone shoes, what am I, your slave?

Knock-Knock!
  Who's there?
Tyson!
  Tyson who?
Tyson garlic
around your neck.
It's the vampire!

Knock-Knock!
  Who's there?
Udder!
  Udder who?
Udder foolishness to keep
reading these jokes!

Nonsense...

Knock-Knock!
  Who's there?
Uphill!
  Uphill who?
Uphill could take your
headache away!

Knock-Knock!
  Who's there?
Urinal!
  Urinal who?
Urinal lot of trouble!

Knock-Knock!
  Who's there?
Vaughn!
  Vaughn who?
Vaughn day you'll stop acting so crazy!

Knock-Knock!
  Who's there?
Vanessa!
  Vanessa who?
Vanessa door going to open?

Knock-Knock!
  Who's there?
Violins!
  Violins who?
  Violins is a bad way
    to settle an
    argument!

Knock-Knock!
　Who's there?
Wales!
　Wales who?
Wales long as I'm here, why don't we go out?

Knock-Knock!
　Who's there?
Walnut!
　Walnut who?
Walnut too sturdy, don't lean on it!

Knock-Knock!
　Who's there?
Wanda!
　Wanda who?
Wanda what you're doing in there!

Knock-Knock!
　Who's there?
Water!
　Water who?
Water you waiting for? Open up!

Hey, Wayne ... Come back!
I was just
kidding.

Knock-Knock!
  Who's there?
Wayne!
  Wayne who?
Wayne, wayne go away!
Come again some other
day!

Knock-Knock!
  Who's there?
Weaken!
  Weaken who?
Weaken still be friends!

Knock-Knock!
  Who's there?
Wendy!
  Wendy who?
Wendy you'll remember—until then, forget it!

Knock-Knock!
  Who's there?
Whenever!
  Whenever who?
Whenever body going to stop asking me that?

Knock-Knock!
  Who's there?
Who!
  Who who?
What, are you an owl all of a sudden?

88

Knock-Knock!
   Who's there?
Whereof?
   Whereof who?
Whereof all the flowers gone?

Knock-Knock!
   Who's there?
Wigwam!
   Wigwam who?
Wigwam your head when it's cold!

It looks so natural.

Knock-Knock!
   Who's there?
William!
   William who?
William make me a sandwich?

Knock-Knock!
  Who's there?
Willy!
  Willy who?
Willy let me on the team or not?

Knock-Knock!
  Who's there?
Wilma!
  Wilma who?
Wilma friends never remember my last name?

Knock-Knock!
  Who's there?
Willow!
  Willow who?
Willow quit it with the knock-knocks already?

Knock-Knock!
  Who's there?
Willow!
  Willow who?
Willow or won't you?

Knock-Knock!
  Who's there?
Window!
  Window who?
Window we leave for school?

Knock-Knock!
    Who's there?
Winston!
    Winston who?
Winston of you guys
threw that paper airplane?

Knock-Knock!
    Who's there?
Wooden!
    Wooden who?
Wooden you rather be playing basketball?

Knock-Knock!
    Who's there?
Woody!
    Woody who?
Woody want, can't you see I'm busy!

Knock-Knock!
    Who's there?
Wylie!
    Wylie who?
Wylie answers the door, the house is burning down!

Knock-Knock!
  Who's there?
X.R.!
  X.R. who?
X.R. great with bacon!

92

Knock-Knock!
  Who's there?
Yachts!
  Yachts who?
Yachts a very good question!

Knock-Knock!
  Who's there?
Yam!
  Yam who?
Yam what I am!

Knock-Knock!
  Who's there?
Yee!
  Yee who?
Hey, are you a cowboy or
what?

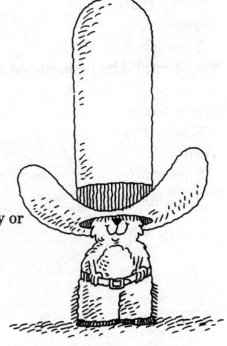

Knock-Knock!
  Who's there?
Yoda!
  Yoda who?
Yoda one who wants to know, so why don't you
guess!

Knock-Knock!
  Who's there?
You!
  You who?
Yes, how can I help you?

Knock-Knock!
  Who's there?
Yugo!
  Yugo who?
Yugo first, I'll be right behind ya!

Knock-Knock!
  Who's there?
Yuri!
  Yuri who?
Yuri up and open the door!

Knock-Knock!
  Who's there?
Zany!
  Zany who?
Zany way to get you to stop with the knock-knocks?

Knock-Knock!
  Who's there?
Zoe!
  Zoe who?
Zoe doesn't recognize
my voice now?

Knock-Knock!
  Who's there?
Enzo Z.!
  Enzo Z. who?
Enzo Z. knock-knock
book!

I thought it would never end!

95

Index

96

96

1. Asleep at the Switch

What would you get if you crossed a camel with a cow?

A lumpy milkshake.

Where does a bull keep his business papers?
In his beef case.

What are the most religious animals?
Holy cows.

Why did the cow cross the street?
To get to the udder side.

What would you get if you crossed a birthday cake with an earthquake?
Crumbs.

Where does candy stay at a hotel?
In a suite.

What colorful letter can you eat?
A brown e.

What did Geronimo say when he jumped out of a plane?
"Me!"

What ailment do pilots experience?
Soars.

Do pilots get colds?
No, flew.

When don't airline employees wear uniforms?
When they are in plane clothes.

Why did the dolphin try to beach itself?
It had no porpoise in life.

What did the girl sea say to the boy sea when he asked for a date?
"Shore."

How do oceans make popcorn?
By microwave.

How does the ocean pay its water bill?
With sand dollars.

How do baseball players keep in contact with friends?

They touch base with them.

What did the baseball glove say to the baseball?

"Catch you later."

Where do catchers eat their dinner?

At home plate.

Where is baseball mentioned in the Bible?

In the big inning.

Where do ghosts sit in the movies?

Dead center.

What does a baby ghost sit in?

A boo-ster chair.

8

What author works on Halloween?
A ghostwriter.

What would you get if you crossed a ghost with
an owl?
*A creature that frightens people and doesn't
give a hoot.*

Why do carpenters take so long to sign
contracts?
They want to hammer out all the details first.

What do you call the female relatives of a house
builder?
Carpenter ants.

Where do carpenters live?
In boarding houses.

Why do carpenters quit their jobs?
They get board.

Why did the bee join the rock band?
To be the lead stinger.

What do bees call their spouses?
"Honey."

How do buzzing insects talk to each other on a
computer?
They use bee-mail.

What do you call a store owned by a bee?
A buzziness.

Which two dogs are opposites?
Hot dogs and chili dogs.

What do you call a pooch with too many ticks?
A watchdog.

What does a dog do that a person steps in ?
Pants.

If every dog has his day, what does a dog with a broken tail have?
A weekend.

Why was Little Miss Muffet upset?
She didn't get her whey.

What's a hamburger's favorite fairy tale?
Hansel and Gristle.

In what factory does Humpty Dumpty work?
In an eggplant.

Why couldn't the three bears get back into their house?
Because it had Goldie locks.

Why did the lion cross the road?
   To get to the other pride.

What would you get if you crossed a lion and a
porcupine?
   *Something you wouldn't want to sit next to on
   the bus.*

Where do lions, tigers, and bears work out?
The jungle gym.

What do lions and tigers prey on?
Their knees.

Why doesn't a banana last long in a household?
Because a banana splits.

Do people like bananas?
Yes, a bunch.

What do you call a banana that has been stepped on?
A banana split.

What's green and goes a hundred miles an hour?
A frog in a blender.

What's a frog's favorite winter game?
Ice hoppy.

What do you call a frog stuck in the mud?
Unhoppy.

Where do you take a frog with poor eyesight?
To the hoptician.

Why did the shoes want to win the race so badly?
They couldn't accept defeat.

Why did the two shoes get along so well?
  They were soul mates.

What did the shoe say to the gum?
  "Stick with me and we'll go places."

Did you hear about the man who walked across the country without shoes?
  It was quite a feat.

What do elephants wear on their legs?
  Elepants.

Why don't elephants play basketball?
They don't look good in shorts.

Why are elephant rides cheaper than pony rides?
Elephants work for peanuts.

Why do people eat chicken eggs and not elephant eggs?
Because everyone hates elephant yolks.

2. Beating around the Bush

What did one hammer say to the other?
"I just broke a nail."

What did the waterfall say to the water fountain?
"You're just a little squirt."

What did one loom say to the other loom?
"Weave me alone."

Why is a new lawyer like an escaped convict?
They both passed their bars.

What do inmates do to amuse themselves in prison?
Sing Sing.

What's the hardest part of grammar for criminals?
The prison sentence.

When do you need to put football players and convicts on the same scale?
When you're weighing the pros and cons.

What animal is the first to rise in the morning?
The early bird.

Do birds memorize their flights?
No, they wing it.

What can you do to help a sick bird?
Get it tweeted.

How do birds get ready to exercise?
They do worm-ups.

What would you get if you crossed a computer with an alligator?
A megabyte.

How does a computer eat?
Maybe a byte here and a byte there.

What animals help computers run?
Rams.

What was wrong with the cleaning lady's computer?
It didn't do windows.

What's the best farm animal for boxing?
Duck!

Why didn't the duck pick up the restaurant check?
  It already had a bill.

If a duck says "Quack, quack" when it walks, what does it say when it runs?
  "Quick, quick."

What do you use to heal a broken duck?
  Duck tape.

What egg is dangerous?
  The eggsecutioner.

What's yellow and black and white?
  Scrambled eggs with salt and pepper.

How does a beach like its eggs?
  Sunny side up.

Why was the car embarrassed?
  It had gas.

Why did the driver throw money on the street?
  So he could stop on a dime.

Why did the battery cross the road?
  It thought it would get a charge out of it.

What help should you seek after buying a rotten used car?
Lemonade.

How do vampires stay healthy?
They take bite-amins.

What do you call a dentist who offers to clean a werewolf's teeth?
Crazy.

What's Dracula's favorite dish?
The quiche of death.

Who do vampires prefer at the circus?
They go for the jugguler.

What do you get when you cross a fat football
player with a pay phone?

A wide receiver.

How many football players does it take to change
a lightbulb?

One, and ten others to recover the fumble.

How does a football coach go fishing?

With his tackle.

What's a couch potato's favorite sport?
Channel surfing.

Why do sheep make bad drivers?
They make too many ewe turns.

What do you call a lamb that fights on the
ocean?
A battlesheep.

How does a sheep protect its driver's license?
It gets it lamb-inated.

What happens when you eat rotten bubble gum?
You get gum disease.

What's a scientist's favorite candy?
Experi-mints.

Why couldn't the girl keep Chicklets in her
mouth?
Because gum drops.

Why isn't it hard to protect children from
cavities?
It's like taking candy from a baby.

What game do ocean waves like to play?
Pitch and toss.

What did the river say to the ocean?
  "It's been nice running into you."

What do you call a teenager who cracks his
knuckles and swims in the ocean?
  A salt-teen cracker.

What do surfers do when the tide goes out?
  Wave goodbye.

What do you call a male bug that floats?
  A buoyant.

What do call a female bug?
  A gallant.

What did one lightning bug say to the other?
  "Give me a push. I think my battery's dead."

What tree catches the most diseases?
  The sycamore.

How does a tree change?
  By turning over a new leaf.

What did the tree say when it couldn't solve the riddle?
  "I'm stumped."

What are sleeping trees called?
  Slumber.

Why was the violinist fired from the orchestra?
He was fiddling around.

Why was the violin so jittery?
It was high-strung.

What bows do violinists use to play their instruments?
Fiddle sticks.

3. Cracking Up

Where does Santa go swimming?
At the North Pool.

What use are skis and sleds?
Snow use.

Does it ever get cold in South America?
   Yes, it can get quite Chile.

What kind of kitchen appliance is the Titanic famous for?
   The sink.

What ice cream drinks weren't found on the Titanic?
   Floats.

How did the escargot cross the ocean?
   By snail boat.

Why do most ships sail the same routes?
   Pier pressure.

What should you do if your ear rings?
   Answer it.

How do ears keep fit?
   With earobics.

What did the mitten say to the thumb?
   "I glove you."

What kind of advice do you get from hands?
   Finger tips.

How do rodents achieve their ambition?
They gopher it.

What is a rodent's favorite amusement park ride?
   The ferret wheel.

What do rodents write on?
   A mouse pad.

What does a doctor do with a sick zeppelin?
   He tries to helium.

What doctor is famous for being lazy?
   Dr. Doolittle.

Why did the leaf go the doctor?
   It was a little green.

What do you call someone who treats sick ducks?
   A ducktor.

How did the farmer find his daughter?
He tractor.

How did the farmer mend his pants?
With a cabbage patch.

Why did the farmer refuse to grow wheat?
It went against the grain.

Why isn't farm land expensive?
It's dirt cheap.

What works best when it has something in its eye?
A sewing needle.

How can you tell when a seamstress is going crazy?
She comes apart at the seams.

What's a seamstress's favorite piece of exercise equipment?
A thread mill.

How was the seamstress after the accident?
On the mend.

How did the pilot buy a present for his wife?
On the fly.

How did the busy track star do his homework?
On the run.

Why was the mortician fired?
He couldn't make his deadlines.

Why was the auto parts salesman fired?
He took too many brakes.

What would you get if you crossed a magician
with a snake?
Abra-ca-cobra!

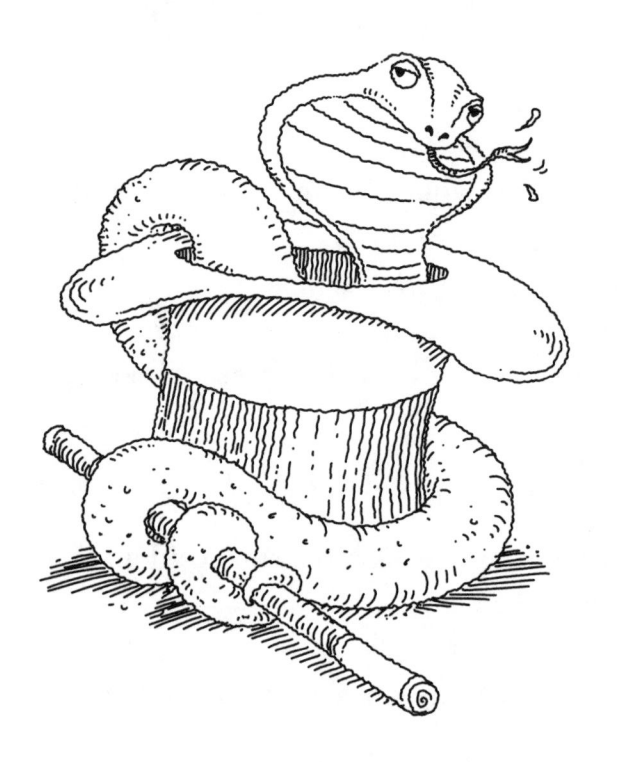

What would you get if you crossed pasta with a boa constrictor?

Spaghetti that winds itself around the fork.

Why did the snake keep checking the tires on his car?

He kept hearing a kind of hiss.

Why did the snake lose its lawsuit?

It didn't have a leg to stand on.

What's yellow on the outside and gray on the inside?

A school bus full of elephants.

Who gives money to elephants who lose a tooth?

The tusk fairy.

Why do elephants have cracks between their toes?

To carry their library cards.

What weighs twelve thousand pounds and is covered with lettuce and special sauce?

A Big MacElephant.

Why did the robber sleep under his bed?

He wanted to lie low.

What do you call a person who steals rubber bands?
A rubber bandit.

What's a thief's favorite metal?
Steel.

Why did the safecracker marry his girlfriend?
They were a good combination.

Why are birds so unhappy in the morning?
Because their little bills are all over dew.

What kind of hat does a bird wear?
A Robin hood.

Why did the bird ask the plastic surgeon for a new nose?
The old one didn't fit the bill.

Why do people feed birds?
For a lark.

What's a guitar player's favorite sport?
Bass ball.

What looks and acts like a male rock star?
A female rock star.

Why wasn't the musical group allowed to play?
They were band.

What's Batman's favorite way to swim?
Bat-stroke.

What's Superman's favorite street?
Lois Lane.

Who taught Superman to tell time?
Clock Kent.

4. Wits End

What does a tennis player use to start a fire?
Tennis matches.

What kind of money do tennis players earn?
Net pay.

What kind of students do letter carriers make?
First class.

What do students wear around their necks?
School ties.

What do class clowns snack on?
Wisecrackers.

What do high school graduates wipe their feet on?
Diploma mats.

Why do mummies like Christmas?
Because of all the wrappings.

What do you call a writer of horror films?
A screamwriter.

What did the papa monster say to his son?
"Father knows beast."

Who is the leader of the popcorn?
The kernel.

What should you say if a farmer wants to talk to you about corn?
"I'm all ears."

Why couldn't the paper doll walk?
It wasn't cut out for it.

Why did the gambler fight with weird people?
He wanted to beat the odds.

Why couldn't Tarzan call Jane?
Her vine was busy.

Why is Scotch Tape so successful?
It has a lot of stick-to-it-ness.

Why don't skiers get ahead in the world?
Because after they get to the top, it's all downhill.

What kind of horse collects stamps?
A hobby horse.

What office did the female horse run for?
Mare.

What has six legs, four eyes, and five ears?
A man riding a horse eating corn.

What should you do if your stallions start to gallop away?
Hold your horses.

What do you call a person who can't flip pancakes?
A flip flop.

What do breakfast eaters do on Saturday nights?
Cereal bowl.

How can you tell that a teapot is angry?
It blows its top.

Why couldn't the instant coffee sue the teapot?
It didn't have the grounds.

What famous fish wears a red, white, and blue hat?
Uncle Salmon.

What do you call a fish without an eye?
A fsh.

Who do fish get to clean their rooms?
  Mermaids.

What dessert do fish serve at parties?
  Crab cakes.

Why don't fish go away for the summer?
Because they are always in school.

If you really like coffee, what train do you take?
An espresso.

What trains carry bubble gum?
Chew chew trains.

Why did the railroad conductor return to his old job?
He wanted to get back on track.

What does a funny train ride on?
A laugh track.

What transportation do chefs prefer?
Gravy trains.

Why wasn't the crooked railroad conductor arrested?
Because he covered his tracks.

What is the laziest vegetable?
The couch potato.

Which vegetables have rhythm?
Beets.

What's a llama's favorite vegetable?
Llama beans.

What vegetable will listen to your problems?
Corn. It's always willing to lend an ear.

What award do they give to wonderful Grandmothers?
Grammies.

What is the smartest mountain?
Mt. Rushmore — it has four heads.

What's the best way to buy holes?
Wholesale.

What should smokers do to quit?
Butt out.

What piece of clothing do you put on an envelope?
  Address.

What's worse than a giraffe with a sore throat?
  An octopus with tennis elbow.

Why do giraffes make good friends?
  They really stick their necks out for you.

Why didn't the bee have extra time?
It was always buzzy.

How do bees brush their hair?
With honeycombs.

If a bee married a rodent, what would its children be called?
Brats.

What language do bees use?
Buzz words.

What does a bee use to cut wood?
A buzz saw.

5. Gags to Riches

What do you call a jail that is specially designed
for baseball sluggers?

The Grand Slammer.

What word is frowned at by baseball players but smiled at by bowlers?

"Strike."

Why do most baseball games have to be played at night?

Because bats sleep during the daytime.

Why are tailors good talkers?

They know how to talk off the cuff.

What did the tailor do when his assistant arrived late for work?
He dressed him down.

Who sails the seven seas and makes good suits?
Sinbad the Tailor.

What's large, yellow, and lives in Scotland?
The Loch Ness canary.

What's yellow and goes "putt, putt, putt"?
A canary playing golf.

How do canaries earn extra money?
By babysitting for elephants on Saturday night.

Why can't Friday beat up Saturday?
Because Friday is a weak day.

What kind of shirt always needs a shower?
A sweatshirt.

What did they wear at the Boston Tea Party?
T-shirts.

What's the best shirt to wear into battle?
A tank top.

Why did the girl protest being expelled for wearing a tank top?
She wanted the right to bare arms.

What kind of dog washes clothes?
  A laundro-mutt.

What do you call the top of a dog house?
  The woof.

What part of a canine helps you find your place
in books?
  Dog ear.

What did the boy say when his puppy ran away
from home?
  "Doggone!"

What do you call someone who steals your
puppy?
  "Doggone thief!"

Why do puppies eat frankfurters?
  Because it's a dog-eat-dog world.

Why do Wall Street investors take only showers?
  They don't want to take a bath in the market.

Why did the businessman buy a herd of cattle?
  His future was at steak.

How did the tailor do in the stock market?
  He lost his shirt.

What do you call it when a police officer quits?
  Cop out.

What happened to Charlie Brown's girlfriend
when she got in trouble with the police?
  *She was carted away in a Peppermint Paddy
  wagon.*

What happened when a hundred hares got loose
on Main Street?
  The police had to comb the area.

How should police officers deal with the public?
Uniformly.

What do you call a flower shop that's burning?
A florist fire.

Do some flowers ride bicycles?
Yes, rose pedals.

What flower believes in past lives?
Rein-carnation.

Why did the writer move from his ranch-style house?
He wanted more than one story.

What would you get if you put butter on your mattress?
A bed spread.

Where should you go to buy a comforter?
Downtown.

What chef thrives under stress?
A pressure cooker.

When does a chef know he's in trouble?
When his goose is cooked.

Why was the gossipy chef fired?
Because he dished out the dirt.

How do you know when a cat burglar has been at your house?
Your cat is missing.

Why was the clumsy cook fired?
She spilled the beans.

Why can you rely on the sun?
It always rises to the occasion.

What did the tree say when spring came?
"What a re-leaf!"

What did the summer say to the spring?
"Help! I'm going to fall."

How did King Kong escape from his cage?
He used a monkey wrench.

How did they train King Kong?
They hit him with a large rolled-up newspaper building.

How do you get a giant into a frying pan?
Use shortening.

Why did the blind man join the navy?
He wanted to go to see.

Why did the talkative man gain so much weight?
Because he liked to chew the fat.

Why did the reporter buy an ice cream cone?
He was desperate for a scoop.

Why did the river go on a diet?
It gained a few ponds.

Why did the rancher get mad when the thief
stole his hay?
   Because it was the last straw.

Why did the cowboy ride his horse to town?
   Because it was too heavy to carry.

Why did the cowboy go to the rodeo?
   Because wild horses couldn't keep him away.

Why did the cattle get upset when the rancher talked about eating beef?
They heard.

How do cattlemen plan for the future?
They make long-range plans.

6. April Fool

What would you get if you crossed a slob with an artist?

A messterpiece.

How do artists become famous?
It's the luck of the draw.

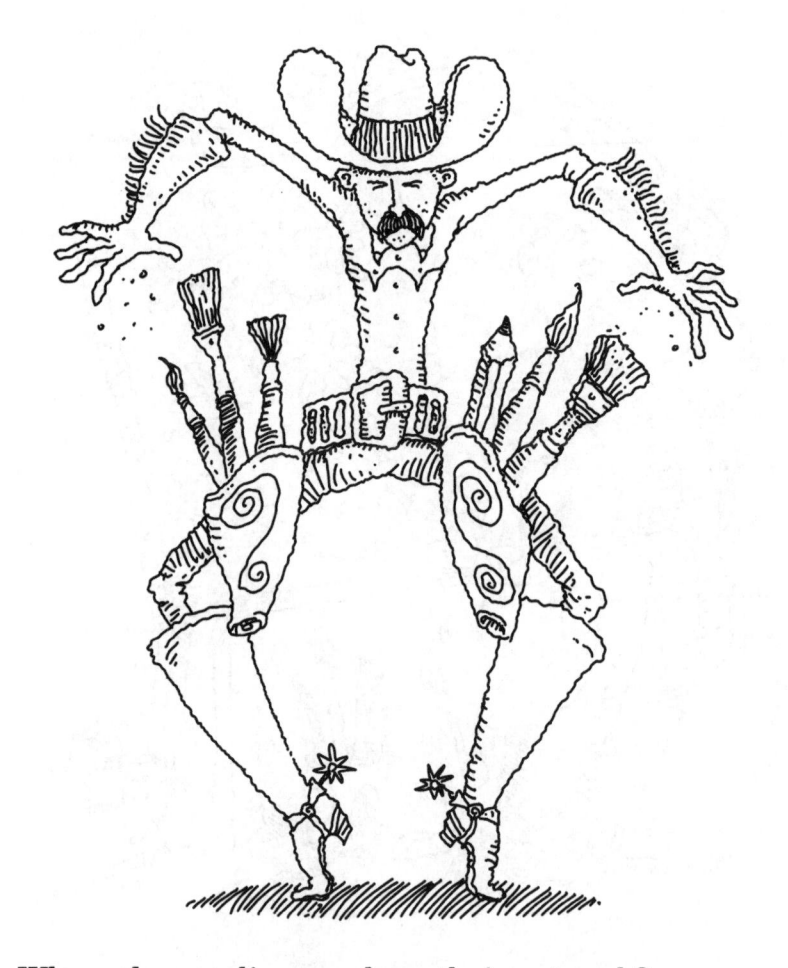

Where do gunslingers show their artwork?
At shooting galleries.

What kind of angel was Noah?
An ark angel.

Why did the angel go to the hospital?
She had harp failure.

Why do the windows in a house of worship have to be cleaned so often?
They're stained glass.

What would you get if you crossed a pig and a porcupine?
A stick in the mud.

What do you call pigs that drive trucks?
Squeals on wheels.

Why did the pig cross the road?
To get ink for his pen.

What do pigs do when they get angry?
They go hog wild.

What's big, lives near the beach, and wears sunglasses?
A two-hundred-pound seagull.

What do you call a beach that keeps losing sand?
A shore loser.

What was the tow truck doing at the racetrack?
Trying to pull a fast one.

Do truck drivers have tough jobs?
  Yes, they have many bumps on the road.

Why did the truck driver's wife divorce him?
  He drove her up the wall.

Why don't rabbits play football?
  Their ears don't fit in the helmet.

How can you find out how big your skunk is?
Use a scent-imeter.

If a skunk wrote a book, what list would it be on?
The best-smeller list.

What animal is the least known?
Anonymouse.

What did the clock say at noon?
"Hands up."

What do you call an attack by a bunch of wigs?
A hair raid.

Do barbers like to dance?
No, they just like to cut in.

Was the man wearing his toupee in the wrong place?
Yes, they pulled the rug out from under him.

How does a wig introduce itself?
"Hair I am."

What do hairdressers do at the end of their lives?
They curl up and dye.

Why didn't the judge have any friends?
He held everyone in contempt.

What did the judge do with the hit-and-run driver?

He sent him to the prison baseball team.

What's a lawyer's favorite meal?

Brief Stroganoff.

When two bullets get married, what do they have?

BB's.

Why did the boulder's wife divorce him?

Because he took her for granite.

How did Benjamin Franklin's wife get rid of him?

She told him to go fly a kite.

Is it hard to be an IRS employee?

Yes, it's very taxing.

Why did the millionaire refuse to move to Alaska?

He didn't want to freeze his assets.

What animal can you borrow money from?

A loan wolf.

What do you call a small tick on the moon?

A moon buggy.

Where do aliens keep their teacups?
On flying saucers.

Why was there no more room for another
astronaut on the space shuttle?
They were outer space.

What would you get if you put a lightbulb in a suit of armor?
A knight light.

Can the king's son write longhand?
No, he prince.

What does the queen do when she gets mad at the king?
She crowns him.

Why did the king think that he could write a book?
He already had a title.

What did the flashlight say to the battery?
"You turn me on."

What's the most dangerous light?
Ultraviolent.

What kind of attention span does a light switch have?
On and off.

What color do nudists prefer?
Buff.

Why didn't the circle enjoy the dance?
It was a square dance.

Why was the inchworm angry?
  It had to convert to the metric system.

What's the most disgusting unit of
measurement?
  Gross.

When is the best time to see a circle?
  When it's around.

What unit of measurement likes to take charge?
  A liter.

What do you call a yo-yo that doesn't come back
up?
  A yo.

What's a counterfeiter's favorite toy?
  Play dough.

What are a writer's least favorite toys?
  Writer's blocks.

Where do spies do their shopping?
  At a snooper market.

What law do hitchhikers abide by?
  The rule of thumb.

What book comes with its own light?
  A matchbook.

What happened when the broom competed against the dustpan?

It was a clean sweep.

What is the rank of an Army dentist?

Drill sergeant.

7. Monkey Business

How do they play basketball in Hawaii?
With a hula hoop.

Why did the basketball player bring a suitcase to the game?
In case he travels.

What do stallions use to fly?
Horse feathers.

What do you call a pony that doesn't whinny?
A little horse.

What public opinion poll do horses like best?
The Gallop Poll.

Why didn't the bird make the curtain call?
He was waiting in the wings.

What did General Bird say to his army?
"Retweet! Retweet!"

What's convenient and weighs two tons?
An elephant six-pack.

Why don't elephants tip bellhops?
They like to carry their own trunks.

Why do elephants have trunks?
Because they can't carry all their stuff in their makeup case.

What would you get if you put 100 pounds of peanuts in an elephant's cage?
  A happy elephant.

Why did the peanut butter jump into the ocean?
  To be with the jellyfish.

Does margarine have wings?
  No, but butterflies.

Why do most cities have the same stores?
It's a mall world.

Where does a lumberjack go to buy things?
To the chop-ing center.

Why did the actress go the bakery?
She was looking for good roles.

Did the actress stop dating the movie star?
Yes, he's out of the picture.

What do models eat off?
Fashion plates.

What do sound waves travel on?
The Earie Canal.

Where do you find bargains at sea?
On sale boats.

What's the most unpleasant boat to travel on?
A hardship.

How did the firefighter quit his job?
In the heat of the moment.

Why did the race car driver quit the circuit?
He wanted to shift gears.

How did the man's new job as a shoe salesman start?

He got off on the wrong foot.

Why didn't the plumber like his job?

He found it draining.

How did the laundry woman look after a day's work?

Washed out.

Where are great dragons remembered?

In the Hall of Flame.

How does a dentist fix a dragon's teeth?

With a fire drill.

What animals are the most computer literate?

Spiders. They practically live on the web.

What do you call it when spiders marry?

Holy weblock.

Why was the spider surprised by the doctor's bill?

It was charged an arm and a leg, an arm and a leg....

Are spiders a global problem?

Yes, as witnessed by the World Wide Web.

What creature helps repair computers?
  Debug.

Where does a turtle go to eat out?
  A slow-food restaurant.

What's green, sour, and weighs over five tons?
  A picklesaurus.

What do you call a pickle that draws?
  A dillustrator.

When do you go on red and stop on green?
  When you're eating watermelon.

What would you get if you put a jar of honey outdoors overnight?
Honey-dew.

What did the man say to the grizzly?
"Bear with me."

What kind of bears enjoy lying in the sun?
Solar bears.

What's the difference between a buffalo and a bison?
You can wash your hands in a bison.

What do you call a llama's mother?
A mama llama.

Why did the banana go to the doctor?
It wasn't peeling well.

Why did the hog go to the eye doctor?
Because of his pig sty.

What illness is caused by the third letter of the alphabet?
C-sickness.

How did the doctor make money?
By ill-gotten gains.

8. Out on a Limb

Why did the talkative photographer take pictures of the steer?

He liked to shoot the bull.

What would you get if you crossed a cow with an octopus?
A farm animal that milks itself.

What would you get if you crossed a parrot with a pig?
A bird that hogs the conversation.

Why do leopards have spotted coats?
Because the tigers bought all the striped ones.

Why is it hard to find a store that will sell leopards coats?
No one wants to wait on them.

Where does a clerk put vile letters?
In the vile cabinet.

Why did the mall store owner bring bongos to the store?
To drum up business.

Why did the store manager hire the cow?
To beef up sales.

How long is a pair of shoes?
Two feet.

What did the zero say to the eight?
"Nice belt."

How do pants address mail to each other?
With zipper codes.

What do farmers do when they make money
selling pigs?
They live high on the hog.

Why couldn't they give the award-winning farmer his prize?
Because he was outstanding in his field.

What did the silly man name his pet zebra?
Spot.

Why did the nineteen kids go to the movies?
The sign out front said "UNDER EIGHTEEN NOT ADMITTED."

What did the mother rope say to her child?
"Don't be knotty."

Why wasn't the sportsman wearing clothes?
He was hunting bare.

What kind of bird hunt is never successful?
A wild goose chase.

What makes a goose different from other animals?
Most animals grow up, but a goose grows down.

Why do people get goose bumps?
Because camel bumps are too big.

What do factory workers and gardeners have in common?
They both do plant work.

What is the most foolish part of a tree?
  The sap.

What furniture is the most entertaining?
  Musical chairs.

What furniture is designed for those who like seedy food and a swim outdoors?
  A birdbath.

Why is a leaking faucet like a racehorse?
  Because it's off and running.

What did the washer say to the drier?
  "Let's go for a spin."

What heating device should really go on a diet?
The potbelly stove.

What do you call a cafeteria after a food fight?
A mess hall.

What do you call someone else's cheese?
Nacho cheese.

Who won first prize at the beauty contest?
The winner.

Who was the biggest liar in the world?
The super duper.

What do you call a fly with no wings?
A walk.

What did the top fly do when the others didn't do their work?
Fireflies.

How do you kill a fly?
Call in the S.W.A.T. team.

On what road do plants travel?
Routes.

Why do bagpipers walk so fast when they play?
To get away from the noise.

What comes after a tuba?
    A three-ba.

Why must you be in good shape to become a
singer?
    You have to be able to carry a tune.

Why did the musical conductor bring the steer
into the orchestra pit?
    He wanted to take the bull by the horns.

Do singers tell you how they feel?
    Only if it's off the record.

What city do sharks come from?
Shark-ago.

Why did the shark spit out the clown?
He tasted funny.

What do you call a whale that talks too much?
A blubber mouth.

What's the favorite dance of sardines?
The can-can.

What sea creature is the biggest celebrity?
A starfish.

Why did the cat put its kittens into a drawer?
It didn't want to leave its litter lying around.

What do hurt cats say?
"Me-OWW!"

What's a cat's favorite dessert?
Chocolate mouse.

How do you get milk from a cat?
Steal its saucer.

9. Rib Ticklers

Why are fast-food restaurants so dangerous?
You might bump into a man eating chicken.

What do you call the wrong meat order at a restaurant?
A miss-steak.

What fat person brings you food in a restaurant?
A weightress.

What's the favorite subject at the South Pole?
Penguinship.

What do good students eat their burgers on?
Honor rolls.

Why did the teacher send the clock to the principal's office?
For tocking too much.

Why did the Fig Newton graduate first in his class?
He was one smart cookie.

How do card sharks walk?
They shuffle.

How does one amoeba talk to another amoeba?
On a cell phone.

Why wouldn't the customer buy fancy rollerblades?
He was a cheapskate.

Why did the customer refuse to buy a bed at first sight?
He wanted to sleep on it first.

Who is the biggest celebrity ever?
The sun. It's a superstar.

Why did the talk show hostess discuss forest fires?
It was a hot topic.

Why did the comedian quit his job?
He was at his wit's end.

Why are set designers difficult?
They make scenes.

What do you call a person with a loose wrist-watch?
Someone with time on his hands.

How does a witch tell time?
With a witchwatch.

What happens when you eat crackers in bed?
You get a crumby night's sleep.

Where do campers snooze when they forget their sleeping bags?
On nap sacks.

Where do athletes like to stay?
In shape.

How can you keep cool at the ball park?
Sit by a fan.

How do hamburgers catch robbers?
With a burger alarm.

Where do you find silverware on a highway?
At the fork in the road.

What's a bat's least favorite hotel?
The cave-inn.

What luggage did the puppy bring on vacation?
A doggie bag.

What kind of luggage always makes a fuss?
Carry-on.

Why are some people afraid to go to the Big Apple?
They believe it's rotten to the core.

What do they use to clean clouds?
  A skyscraper.

How do successful weathermen get ahead?
  They take the world by storm.

What has five eyes and sleeps in a water bed?
  The Mississippi river.

What would you get if you crossed a monster
with a heavy rainstorm?
  A horrorcane.

Why were the bones chasing the skull?
  They wanted to get ahead.

What would you get if you threw Daffy Duck into
the Atlantic Ocean?
  Saltwater Daffy.

What did St. Nicholas build when he wanted a
place to put his clothes?
  A Santa Closet.

What flies through the air and is covered with
syrup?
  Peter Pancake.

What do you call a supernatural being with a
tan-colored rabbit?
  Genie with the light brown hare.

What's Tarzan's favorite Christmas song?
"Jungle Bells."

Who is the Pied Piper's poor brother?
The Pied Pauper.

Is it possible to lose your television clicker?
It's a remote possibility.

How did the gymnast watch television?
She flipped through the channels.

What's the most confusing part of the week?
Week daze.

Why was the lumberjack so successful?
   Don't ax.

Why couldn't the lumberjack keep up with his work?
   He was backlogged.

What did the mental health worker carry instead of a briefcase?
   A basket case.

What do you call polite butlers and maids?
   Civil servants.

10. Tickled Pink

What are the chances of an artist making a living?
They're sketchy.

Why did the sculptor think he was going crazy?
He lost his marbles.

What happened when the artist threw a
tantrum?
He showed his true colors.

Why don't foreign ambassadors get sick?
They have diplomatic immunity.

Where does the president of the birds live?
In the West Wing.

Which one of your teeth is always nice and
polite?
Your sweet tooth.

Why did the guy use the daily paper for Kleenex?
He had a nose for news.

What part of your body is a real loser?
Defeat.

What kind of teeth can't be trusted?
False teeth.

What part of a letter carrier's anatomy is the
first to go?
Deliver.

What's a computer's favorite snack?
Micro-chips.

What do you call brilliant Internet users?
Star tekkies.

What did the computer program and the itchy dog have in common?
They both had bugs.

Why did the computer hacker refuse to kill spiders?
Because he needed the web sites.

What do you call computer correspondence with a mouse?
Eeek-mail.

What do you say to speed up a turtle?
"Make it snappy."

What time do crocodiles meet their dates?
Date o'croc.

What cell phones do lizards use?
A repdial.

Why did the unhappy nun refuse to leave her job?
It's hard to quit the habit.

Why are mosquitoes religious?
First they sing over you and then they prey on you.

Why did the fish go to the priest?
Because confession is good for the sole.

Why did the fungi leave the party early?
Because there wasn't mushroom.

What's red and goes "putt, putt, putt?"
An outboard apple.

If an apple a day keeps the doctor away, what does an onion a day do?
It keeps everyone away.

What would you get if you crossed a water balloon with a needle?
Wet.

What would you get if you crossed a belt, a strawberry, and a shark?
Buckleberry Finn.

What's black and white and green?
A seasick zebra.

What's black and white and very dangerous?
A zebra on a skateboard.

Where do Arabs leave their camels when they go shopping?
In a camelot.

Are deer rebellious?
  Yes, they always try to buck the system.

What do you call a near-collision of two dresses?
  A clothes call.

What did the firefighter wear to work?
  A blazer.

What crime was the celery arrested for?
  Stalking.

Why did the bad check writer continue his crimes after jail?
He wanted to forge ahead.

What makes a loaf of bread happy?
Being kneaded.

What do bread bakers do on their day off?
Loaf.

What do geeks and nerds eat?
Square meals.

What side dish does a miner eat?
Coal slaw.

How can you give up cooking Thanksgiving dinner?
Go cold turkey.

What do people call chickens in prison?
Henmates.

Why was the hen so arrogant?
She had a large eggo.

What is a duck's favorite snack?
Quacker jacks.

What kind of test is the most irritating?
The cross examination.

Why did the school principal fire the lazy phys ed teacher?
Because he didn't work out.

What should a teacher do when a deer gets an "A" on a test?
Pass the buck.

How does a gym teacher travel?
He flies coach.

What do you call two witches who live together?
Broom mates.

How do witches break the sound barrier?
With a sonic broom.

Why was the baby ant so confused?
Because all of his uncles were ants.

What would you get if you crossed a robot with a skunk?
R 2 PU.

What do scientists do when they lose their keys?
Research.

What kind of weights do beginning bodybuilders use?
Paperweights.

What cup can't you drink from?
A hiccup.

What word has the most letters in it?
Mailbox.

Index

Contents

Library of Congress Cataloging-in-Publication Data

10 9 8 7 6 5 4 3 2 1

Published by Sterling Publishing Company, Inc.
387 Park Avenue South, New York, N.Y. 10016
© 2001 by Charles Keller
Distributed in Canada by Sterling Publishing
℅ Canadian Manda Group, One Atlantic Avenue, Suite 105
Toronto, Ontario, Canada M6K 3E7
Distributed in Great Britain and Europe by Chris Lloyd
463 Ashley Road, Parkstone, Poole, Dorset, BH14 0AX, England
Distributed in Australia by Capricorn Link (Australia) Pty Ltd.
P.O. Box 6651, Baulkham Hills, Business Centre,
NSW 2153, Australia

Pierce
Super Silly
Riddles

CHARLES
KELLER

**Illustrated by
Dave Winter**

Sterling Publishing Co., Inc.
New York

Double Twist

KINGFISHER
a Houghton Mifflin Company imprint
222 Berkeley Street
Boston, Massachusetts 02116
www.houghtonmifflinbooks.com

First published in 2007
2 4 6 8 10 9 7 5 3 1

LIBRARY OF CONGRESS CATALOGING-IN-PUBLICATION DATA
has been applied for.

ISBN-13: 978-0-7534-6023-8

Printed in India
1TR/0906/THOM/SCHOY/60BNWP/C

Double Twist

DONNA KING

KINGFISHER
BOSTON

Chapter 1

"Most kids spend their summer holiday sunbathing on a beach in Spain," Jack Lee muttered to his younger sister Laura. "So how come you're standing here shivering at the side of an ice rink?"

"Because I'm a child star!" Laura said with a grin. "A genius on ice!"

Jack zipped his jacket up to his chin. "Says who?"

"Says Mum." Laura waited impatiently for the public session to end so that she could skate onto the ice for her private coaching lesson with Vera Mozer while Jack went to play soccer. Their mum was due to pick her up later. "Where's Patrick?" Jack wondered out loud.

"Don't worry—he'll be here." Laura watched the little kids on the ice. They whizzed around the rink like demons, in and out of the grown-ups, who wobbled and crashed down like dominoes. One or two older kids tried out turns and spins, taking the whole thing more seriously. "Patrick's never late," she added.

Jack glanced back at the entrance, spied Laura's tall, serious ice-dancing partner, and yelled out his name. "Hey, Patrick, over here!" Now he could dash.

Patrick joined them. He was wearing a thick padded jacket and a scarf wound high around his neck. "Hey," he said quietly.

"Where are your folks?" Jack asked.

"Mum and Dad? They dropped me off and then went to the bank. They'll be back in a few minutes."

"So is it okay if I head off?"

Laura and Patrick nodded. Laura was grinning at the sight of another grown-up biting the dust. A middle-aged woman squealed as she went down, smack on her bottom. "Oops!"

"Don't laugh!" Patrick bit his lip and looked away.

"She's down! Now she's up and brushing the ice off herself. . . . Oops, she's down again!" Eventually, the poor woman made it to the edge of the rink and clung onto the rail. "Why isn't she at home watching TV and knitting woolly scarves for her grandkids?"

"Laura!" Patrick shook his head, glad when the siren sounded for everyone to clear the ice. At least now Laura wouldn't be able to make fun of the old ladies.

"Lighten up!" Laura giggled, saying hi to a couple of kids she knew from school as they came off the ice. "Hey, Georgina! Hey, Abi!"

"Are you here to practice?" Abi asked as she bent down to take off her skates.

"Yep. Why?"

"Just wondered if you wanted to join us at the café."

"Thanks. I'd love to, but we've got a big competition coming up. Gotta keep on practicing those twizzles!"

"Poor you!" Abi grinned. "Where are you jetting off to this time?"

"Montreal, in just under a month."

"Canada?" Abi's jaw dropped. "Wow!"

"Junior Grand Prix," Patrick chipped in. "We're in the running for a medal if we work hard."

Georgina tugged on her friend's arm. "C'mon—I'm starving!"

"Well, good luck!" Abi said to Laura and Patrick. "Wow, Canada . . . cool!"

"Laura, you need more leg and foot extension in that third section!" Vera's eagle eyes didn't miss a thing. "Patrick, you were too close to the boards on the synchronized leg swing!"

"Sorry!" Laura told her partner under her breath. They'd been working nonstop for an hour, and her concentration was beginning to dip. "This compulsory section isn't my thing."

"We've still got to get it right," he insisted. "Let's do it one more time."

They took up their positions in the center of the empty rink. Their coach watched from the barrier. "I'm asking a lot of you with this paso doble," she called. "You have to dance exactly to the beat and keep the Latin spirit going, while getting those twizzles right and leading smoothly into the lift at the same time. Okay, try again!"

Laura heard the music start. She noticed Patrick's mum and dad behind Vera and then her own mum joining them. With this audience, she knew she'd better get her act together. *Leg and foot extension!* she reminded herself. *Synchronized leg swings!*

Together, she and Patrick sprang into action. This rhythm was tricky—it was fast and dramatic, and if you missed a beat, the whole thing went wrong.

"Laura, your foot was loose on that diagonal sequence. Patrick, you overrotated on the landing of that double throw loop!" Once more Vera picked up every tiny error and bellowed out across the ice. It was what you'd expect from a woman who had been an Olympic ice-dancing gold-medal winner herself. She never let you get away with one single thing.

Laura linked hands with Patrick for another lift, using their speed to get her off the ground and spreading her arms wide as he hoisted her into the air. She saw the overhead lights start to blur as Patrick spun her; she remembered her leg and foot extension and felt herself lowered and her blades make contact with the ice.

"Good!" Vera called.

Laura made eye contact with her partner and grinned. *Definite praise from the great ex-champion—wow!*

They got their leg lines sorted out on the next turn sequence and then made their grand finish, arms flung wide, backs arched like Spanish bullfighters.

"Whoa!" Laura gasped. She relaxed her position and gave her mum a quick wave. "Patrick, I think we just did the whole thing without one mistake!"

He nodded happily, his gray eyes gleaming, waving at his own mum and dad as he and Laura skated toward Vera to hear her verdict.

Their coach gave them a hard look from underneath her fur hat, standing with her hands in her pockets and clicking her tongue against the roof of her mouth. "Not bad," she said slowly in her thick accent. "But not the best. Now, go and do it all over again!"

Chapter 2

"Read me a story!" Laura's little sister, Imogen, plonked down on the sofa beside her and thrust a big picture book under her face.

"Not now, Immy. I'm tired." And bruised and battered from a fall that she'd taken at the end of their latest coaching session. She and Patrick hadn't timed a lift correctly, and she'd crashed to the ice doing what felt like 30 miles per hour. Now all she needed was some hot chocolate and TV.

"Puh-lease!" Immy begged, her five-year-old face screwing up into a soulful expression. "It's about a giant with a bad headache—look!"

"I've got a bad headache all of my own!" Laura sighed, giving in and taking the book. "'George the giant woke up one morning with a giant headache,'" she read, while Immy stared at the pictures. "'He got out of his giant bed and put on his giant slippers . . .'"

". . . and took a giant aspirin and lived happily ever after!" Laura's younger brother, James, babbled, his mouth full of cereal. He came and snatched the book. "Cut the giant stuff, Laura—I'm trying to watch TV!"

Immy gave a high wail and ran off to tell their dad. Jack snatched the remote control and flicked through until he found a soccer game.

"Happy families!" Laura grinned, stretching out on the sofa and testing out her bruises. In her head she was going through the routine that she and Patrick would have to practice tomorrow—a smooth and silky salsa changing to a slower rumba and then back to the salsa. With luck, her bruises wouldn't hurt too much. "Ouch!" she groaned as she pressed a tender spot.

Then Immy came back to practice trampolining on the sofa, and Jimmy had a fight with Jack about the remote control.

If we fall on that curved lift, we have to get up and keep skating! Laura reminded herself, getting up from the sofa and silently going through the motions of the routine in a kind of crazy mime. *And we don't skate through the music—we keep to the beat!*

"Where's my giant book?" Immy clamored, bouncing up and down.

"Give me that remote!" Jimmy yelled.

"Goal!" Jack roared, punching the air with his fist.

Tony Lee walked in on the chaos. "Good God!" he muttered. One daughter was wrecking the sofa. The other had her legs in the air like a lunatic. The two boys were threatening to maim each other for life. "It's a miracle how anyone survives in this house!"

And he turned right around and disappeared into his office.

"Dinnertime!" the kids' mum yelled from the kitchen. "Immy, Jimmy, Laura, Jack—come and eat!"

It was only in bed that night that Laura finally wound down. She'd been on the move since six, with her early-morning coaching session, followed by shopping with Abi, followed by taking Immy to the park, followed by her afternoon training session with Vera. But that was a normal summer day for Laura—sprinting from this to that, dreaming of Montreal.

We can win a medal! she told herself, snuggled under her covers, staring up at the dark ceiling. *Okay, so we have to beat the Americans and the Italians, not to mention the Canadian and Russian couples, but our routines are great on content, thanks to Vera, and it's up to Patrick and me to get our technique perfect during the next two weeks.*

Though Laura's body was finally resting, her mind would not switch off. *I can't believe I'm going to Canada! Of course, I've seen it on TV—snow on the Rocky Mountains and everything. And I've been to lots of places already—Bulgaria and the Czech Republic, plus London lots of times, which is amazing. But I've never been to Montreal!*

Laura heard her dad come upstairs, switching off the lights as he went. She heard the bedroom door open and close.

Go to sleep! she told herself. . . . *Maybe we'll get a medal!* she thought, her head in a whirl. *We were fourth in Andorra, just behind the Italians. Our three programs are better this time. If we skate really well, I'm sure we can get a medal! And if we don't, so what?*

For a while Laura lay still, trying to picture the event in Montreal. She saw pairs of skaters in beautiful costumes—some in bright scarlet and gold, some in pale blue, others in white and silver, turquoise and purple. She saw the bright lights shining down on the pure-white ice, heard the music begin for her and Patrick . . .

If we don't win, we'll still have a really cool time, she told herself. *We'll skate as well as we can and have fun. I mean, what could be better than arriving in Canada with Vera, putting in our last training sessions, and then getting out there in front of all those people?*

The question floated in the darkness.

Nothing! she answered, finally turning over and getting ready to sleep. *There is nothing in this whole world better than being on the ice with Patrick, skating our dream!*

"Try the step sequence again," Vera ordered. "Patrick, your right foot is still weaker than your left. Laura, you need more body contact with Patrick!"

Salsa! Snaky hips, back bends, and arm flicks. Laura danced to the music, working in a tricky combination of steps across the

17

ice. She was tired this morning because she hadn't slept well the night before, but she still threw herself into the training session with every ounce of energy she had. *If you're gonna do something, do it one hundred percent—da-da-duh-dah!*

"Okay, come over here," Vera called after they'd completed the sequence.

Laura let go of Patrick's arm and skated smoothly to the barrier.

"You were late for the second twizzle," Patrick muttered as he followed.

Laura frowned. She was sure that she hadn't been late. "No, you were *early*," she mumbled back.

Just lately she and Patrick had been having these little squabbles. He was always finding faults, and she was too feisty to let it pass.

"You were late," he insisted, skating to a halt in front of Vera.

"Patrick, don't skate ahead of the music," their coach told him. "And try to

18

look like you're having fun!"

He looked down at the ice, breathing hard and trying to catch his breath. Laura said nothing, but she thought, *I told you so!*

"Listen," Vera went on, her breath clouding the cold air. "The salsa section has to be fun to do and fun to watch—otherwise, forget it. Then, when you slow down for the rumba section, when the trumpet comes in, you must look at each other—skate as if you are in love!"

Laura watched Patrick's face. He blushed and coughed, as if clearing his throat. *Oh, no, the "love" word!*

"Patrick, do you hear what I'm saying?"

"Yeah," he muttered, looking as if he wanted the ice to melt and swallow him.

Lighten up! Laura tried not to giggle. *It's not as if Vera's actually telling you to love me in real life!* The idea made the embarrassed laugh rise to the surface. *I mean, we've been skating together since we were eight!*

"Don't be shy," the coach continued in

her deep Russian voice. "Enjoy!"

"Should we do it again?" Laura was revving up, ready to go, tightening her ponytail and pushing back strands of her dark hair.

Vera looked hard at Patrick. "No, we'll take a break. Come, sit!"

They skated off the ice and sat on a bench, listening to their coach's advice.

"Laura, you look tired today. You need to get more sleep. Patrick, you are skating with the weight of the world on your shoulders. Go away from here and have fun."

"I'd rather practice some more," he said, sitting hunched forward with his knees wide apart and his hands clasped. His gray eyes were worried. "We've got less than four weeks to go."

"Is something the matter?" Vera picked up a problem and, as usual, got straight to the point. "Tell me. Is it your father?"

Patrick took a deep breath. "He's

putting pressure on me at home," he admitted. "He's on my case all the time—practice more, eat right, build up your strength, blah-blah!"

"Wow!" Laura thought of her own dad—so laid-back that he almost fell over. If anything, it was her mum who pushed Laura on to succeed.

"Your father is right," Vera insisted. "All these things are important. But you must also have a life outside skating. Go to a movie, chill out."

Laura's eyes widened in surprise. Was she hearing right?

"I mean it," Vera said, looking at her watch and discovering that it was time for the ice rink to open up to the public. She took off her big fur hat to reveal a helmet of flattened blonde hair. "So, we all want a medal in Montreal more than we've ever wanted anything in our whole lives. We want to go there and show that we are the best, right?"

Laura and Patrick nodded, aware that the first skaters were arriving on the ice. Laura saw Abi and waved.

"We are good," Vera insisted. "We have worked hard all summer. We have a fabulous program for you to skate."

Level-four lifts, serpentine steps, combination spins . . . Laura knew for sure that these things would impress the Montreal judges.

"But, Patrick, the fun is not there for you. And too much pressure means you make mistakes."

"So can somebody tell me how you make yourself relax?" he muttered, seeing his mum and dad in the distance and standing up from the bench.

"Just come to my house for the day," Laura joked. "My brother Jack can give you lessons in chilling out, no problem!"

Patrick didn't smile. Instead, he took off his skates and went to join his parents.

"Hmm," Vera said, shaking her head. "That boy!"

"I know," Laura agreed. *Way too serious, way too uptight*.

She looked at the rink, now crowded with people having fun. Okay, so some of them could hardly skate a step, but they were laughing as they fell over and their friends pulled them back up onto their feet.

"See you tomorrow morning, early," Vera told her, heading for the exit.

"See you," Laura replied. She spotted a tiny kid zooming over the ice, followed by his nervous dad. Then two cool girls around the same age as her, looking good and knowing it in their bright, slinky tops, showing off in front of the boys.

A group of noisy kids skated behind the two girls for one full circuit around the ice, until one boy broke away and decided to do some showing off of his own. He put on a burst of speed to find a clear patch of ice and then started a spin—slow at first and then, tucking his arms across

23

his chest, getting faster and faster.

Wow! Laura thought. *He can skate!*

The boy, who was maybe 13 or 14, came out of the spin and struck out across the path of the two girls, putting in a couple of turns. He was laughing and calling to his friends, who jostled and kidded him.

"Hey, Scott!" one called. "Show Alexa and Hannah that hip-hop thing!"

He laughed and began to pose with his arms, picking up a rhythm with his feet.

"Show-off!" the first girl said, flicking back her hair.

"Scott Yorke, you're so-o-o not clever!" the second scoffed.

I don't know about that, Laura thought, looking with a well-trained eye. *I'd say he was pretty neat. Good rhythm, smooth steps.*

The boy shrugged, put in another turn, and then skated off into the crowd.

Laura watched him disappear—a tall, sporty kid with short black hair, wearing a cool T-shirt and jeans.

"You can say one thing for sure," Laura said with a sigh, thinking of Patrick and turning away from the ice. "That hip-hop kid knows how to have fun!"

Chapter 3

"Everything okay?" Laura's mum asked early the following morning.

Helen Lee got up at five o'clock every day except Sunday, winter, spring, summer, and fall, to make sure that Laura got to the ice rink on time. Somehow she managed to be bright and cheerful, even at that time of day.

"Yeah, ready," Laura said, grabbing a last mouthful of toast and a quick gulp of orange juice.

"Tony, make sure Immy gets up in time for her doctor's appointment at nine!" Helen called upstairs. "She's having her ears checked, remember. And kick Jack out at seven for his paper route. Oh, and

Jimmy is going to Adam's house this morning. Adam's mum says to drop him off at nine-thirty. . . . "

There was no reply from the bedroom, but Laura knew that her dad' would somehow manage to get everything sorted out. She got into the car, ready to doze on the way to the rink.

"How are you feeling?" her mum asked as they drove through the deserted streets.

"Good."

"Not too nervous about the Grand Prix?"

"Nope." *Z-z-z-z-z*.

"How about Patrick?"

"Patrick's Patrick—you know."

"How does Vera think you'll do in Montreal?"

"Depends." *Z-z-z-z*. "Mum, no more questions—let me sleep, okay?"

Laura dozed off, and before she knew it, they were pulling up in the empty parking lot, where there was only last night's litter blowing in the morning breeze and a few pigeons pecking at someone's abandoned burger and fries. *Charming!*

"Are you staying or going?" she asked her mum.

"Staying." Helen handed Laura her sports bag. "I'm not working until noon today. It'll be good to see how you're doing."

"Mum, we're doing great!" Laura protested. Today she felt like she could do without the extra pressure of being watched. "I hope you're not turning into Patrick's mum and dad!"

Helen laughed. "'Tell me, Vera, is Laura working as hard as she should?'" She copied Mrs. Cole's prim voice.

"Yeah, whatever!" Smiling, Laura swung in through the main door and went to get changed, brushing her hair back from her face and putting on tights and a red practice top and skirt. She carried her skates under her arm as she headed for the rink.

By now, Patrick was there, for once minus his mum and dad. Vera, too, was waiting.

"Hey," Laura said, quickly putting on her skates. "Are you okay?" she asked him.

He nodded. "I'm kind of tired," he admitted. "Not enough sleep last night."

"Me neither." Laura saw his pinched face and decided that he was still stressed out.

Vera stepped in. "Today I think we should concentrate on our rumba section for the original program. Okay, go ahead."

"Oops, this is the part I'm worried about," Laura admitted. It was the so-called romantic section, where she and Patrick had to be lovey-dovey.

"*You're* worried!" he said and sighed. "Dad's already been on my back today—I don't skate fast enough, I'm not throwing high enough, blah-blah, yackety-yack!

She grinned. "Yeah, he's like Vera—nothing's ever good enough!" Across the rink, their coach was talking to her mum.

"Better put on a good performance then," she said as she and Patrick took to the ice.

Take the center of the rink, hold Patrick's hand, wait for the music to start. Look completely confident!

The opening notes for the rumba floated across the ice. The two women came close to the barrier to watch every move.

"Okay?" Laura muttered under her breath.

Patrick nodded, his face tense and pale.

Hold hands and glide forward smoothly, picking up speed. Skate as close to the barrier as we can, swoop around in a wide arc, prepare for the first lift!

Their blades sliced through the smooth, glistening surface of the ice, sending up a cold, white powder. They moved fast, and Patrick prepared to take Laura's weight on his right shoulder. She felt herself rise high up in the air, flung her arms out wide, arched her back, and flew.

Behind the barrier, Helen Lee applauded the lift while Vera took notes.

Land smoothly, without a jolt, stay balanced, wait for Patrick to catch up. . . . We did it!

The nerve-racking lift was over. Laura could relax.

The music played on; a trumpet sounded slow and soulful. But Patrick was half a beat off tempo, skating slightly behind her.

He's tired, Laura reminded herself, waiting for him to catch up before they sped across the center of the rink and went into their synchronized double twist and then a lift.

No problem—we can do this! she thought. *We've done it a thousand times before!*

Once more Patrick needed to use their speed to lift her. He threw her into the air, spinning her high, speeding close to the barrier where their stern coach stood—so close, in fact, that the back edge of his left skate clicked against the metal board.

Laura heard the click as she landed. She glanced around to see her partner struggling to stay balanced. His arms flew wide, and he leaned backward, his skates churning up the ice. Then he lost it and toppled against the barrier, landing in a heap as the high trumpet notes played on.

He's down! He's not getting up to restart. He's not even moving! Quickly, Laura broke out of the routine and skated back toward Patrick. "What happened?" she cried, bending over him.

"It's my knee!" he groaned, his face white and his mouth twisted in pain.

"Stay still—don't move!" Vera yelled as she strode onto the ice. She checked the knee and then shook her head. "You dislocated the joint," she told him. "We need to get you straight to the hospital."

Laura crouched on the ice beside him. "Don't worry—you'll be okay," she whispered, as if by saying it she could hang onto their dream.

"What about Montreal?" Patrick gasped, the pain still showing on his face.

Yeah, the Junior Grand Prix—my and Patrick's big chance! Laura looked anxiously at their coach.

Vera sighed and gave it to them straight. "You can forget it," she said firmly. "I can tell you now, Patrick—no way is this leg injury going to heal in time!"

Helen Lee called Mr. and Mrs. Cole, who arrived at the rink at the same time as the ambulance that was taking their son to the hospital. They met up in the empty lot, where Laura and Vera watched the paramedics carry the stretcher away.

Mrs. Cole rushed straight to her son, while Mr. Cole approached Vera. "How bad is it?" he asked.

"Pretty bad." Vera hadn't held back before, and she didn't now. "They'll have to X-ray the knee and push the joint back into position."

"How long will it take to get better?"

Vera shrugged. "We don't know how much damage has been done to the ligaments. Also, the bone might be cracked."

Laura shivered as the ambulance door

closed behind Patrick. She relived the moment when the accident had happened, wishing with all her might that life was something that you could rewind to a certain point before things went wrong and then start all over again.

Mr. Cole shook his head in disbelief and then glanced at Laura. "Whose fault was this?"

"Nobody's fault, Mr. Cole," Vera said firmly. "Patrick had an unlucky accident, that's all. It happens in ice-skating."

"It couldn't be a worse time." Patrick's father fretted as his wife came to talk to him.

"We have to follow the ambulance," she told her husband.

"I'll come too," Vera decided, quickly saying good-bye to Laura and Helen. "I'm so sorry this has happened!" she told them quietly, for once dropping her stern front and letting her emotions show. "I had high hopes for Montreal and my little Laura!"

For the first time, Laura felt the tears

coming. She sniffed them back. "Me, too," she murmured. It was weird what happened when a dream was shattered—you were left feeling shocked and empty, until someone told you that they were sorry. Then the tears put in an appearance.

"Come on," her mum said, taking her by the arm. "Let's get you home."

"There'll be other chances," Tony Lee told his daughter.

Laura had moped around the house all day, taking in the news from the hospital that Patrick's kneecap was actually broken, as well as pushed out of place.

"That's that," her mum had said before she'd left for work. "There's no chance of him being ready to skate for at least three months."

That's that. Finished. End of story. Laura had drifted from room to room, ignoring Immy's demands to play a game of Twister. The afternoon had passed by in a dull daze.

But now her dad had sat her down and

started giving her advice.

"Listen, honey, I know this must hurt. You'd built your hopes up so high about going to Canada and winning a medal. But life doesn't always work out the way we want it to."

Why doesn't it? Laura thought. *Patrick and I worked all year for this. It's just not fair!*

"Laura, are you listening?"

She nodded. "Yeah, Dad. Sorry."

"Like I said, there'll be another chance. Just give Patrick's leg time to heal and then start again."

"It'll be too late," she said and sighed. "We'll slip way down the rankings. No one will even look at us the next time we enter a competition."

"Of course they will. You two are very talented skaters. There's no way that's going to change."

At last Laura managed to look up. It wasn't her father's usual style to hand out praise. He said it was in case she got too bigheaded. "Do you mean that, Dad? Do you really think we're talented?"

He grinned. "Big-time!"

"Wow! Suddenly I feel loads better."

"Good." Her dad patted her on the knee and then left to find out why Immy was wailing and knee-deep in feathers up in her bedroom. "What happened to your pillow?" Laura heard him say.

Okay, she said to herself. *Enough feeling sorry for yourself! What about poor Patrick? Note to self—better visit him tomorrow.*

"Hey, tough news about Patrick, kiddo!" Jack said, poking his head around the door. "But look at it this way—no more early-morning workouts!"

Laura managed to smile.

A few minutes later, Jimmy came in to flick on the TV. He glanced at Laura. "Jack said you were blubbering about not going to Canada!"

"I'm so-o-o not!" she protested, getting up and whacking him with a cushion.

"Anyway, who says I'm not going?"

"You can't go if you don't have a partner, dummy!"

Laura frowned. Suddenly she wanted to fight back. "Who says I don't have a partner?"

Jimmy turned up the volume. "Patrick broke his leg, dumbo!"

"So . . . maybe I can find a new one."

"Da-dah-di-dah!" Jimmy blocked his ears.

Giving up, Laura flounced out of the room. Okay, so she knew better than to expect sympathy from Jimmy. But, hey, what had she just said? *Maybe I can find a new partner.*

Laura stopped in the hallway and thought about it. *A new partner. Where? How?*

Don't be stupid—there's only a month to go before Montreal. How can you find someone new?

"There must be a kid who can skate around here somewhere," she murmured.

Go on then. Go ahead—perform a miracle and find him!

Laura shook her head to get rid of the doubting voice. "You think I can't perform miracles? Just watch me!"

So, you find the boy wonder, the new, undiscovered skating genius. But how is he going to learn the routines in time?

She shook her head again. "Shut up!" she told the nuisance voice. "You know me. If I set my heart on doing something, I do it!"

"Talking to yourself?" Jack asked as he flew downstairs three steps at a time and vanished into the kitchen.

"What are you up to, Laura?" her dad asked, standing with a feather-covered Immy at the top of the stairs.

Laura looked up at him with a determined light in her eye. "I'm going to the ice rink," she told him, without stopping to explain. "Don't worry—I'll be back home by seven!"

Chapter 4

On Friday night the ice rink was always humming. The skaters were mostly kids. There were hardly any grown-ups. Laura lined up to get in, impatient to get through the turnstile and onto the ice.

"Let's get a Big Mac after we finish here," the boy in front said to his friends, glancing back at Laura. "Hey, aren't you . . . ?"

"Yeah, she's the girl who does the fancy routines before they let the riffraff in," his friend said.

Laura shrugged and tried to turn away, but now everyone started to recognize her.

"What are you training for? Are you really famous?" one girl in the line wanted to know.

"How do you do all those spin things?" another asked.

At last it was Laura's turn to pay. Quickly, she handed over her money and slipped through the turnstile, heading straight for the ice, where all of her awkwardness fell away. After all, while she was skating, no one could get at her.

For a while she glided across the smooth surface, swerving between other skaters, soaking up the sights and sounds, just chilling. This felt good, she decided—being one of the crowd, feeling happy, no worries.

But then she remembered why she had come. *You're here to be a talent scout*, she reminded herself. *There's got to be someone here who's a cool skater. Okay, so maybe he won't be trained—maybe he'll just be here to have fun. But he'll have real talent!*

As Laura began to look around, her hopes of working a miracle were soon dented. For a start, as usual there were

more people falling over than skating
smoothly. Some would take a few faltering
steps and then lose their balance; others
would wobble on for longer and then
crash against the barrier, unable to stop.
Their friends would pull them up from
the ice and drag them on.

Huh! Laura frowned and skated,
threading her way between the laughing
knots of kids. *Where's that kid I saw before?
The one they called Scott? I thought he'd be
here on a Friday night.*

But she couldn't pick out his dark hair
and cool T-shirt, and she had to
concentrate hard to steer clear of the
tumbling, toppling bodies that littered the
ice. After half an hour she was ready to
give up and head for home.

"Watch out!" A cry came from behind,
and a figure hurtled toward her.

Laura swerved to avoid a crash. The boy
was out of control, on a collision course
with the barrier.

"Ouch!" Laura grimaced as she anticipated the sudden stop.

"Oof!" The boy hit the barrier and knocked the breath from his body. Soon he was surrounded by half a dozen of his friends, who were picking him up and dusting him off.

"Stand up, Will! . . . Man, you hit that wall hard! . . . Can you breathe? . . .Will, talk to us!"

"Okay, cool—I'm good!" At last the boy got back on his feet, and the crowd surrounding him melted away, leaving only the one person that Laura had been looking for.

Scott's here! Wow, this is my lucky night!

"Do you want to stay or leave?" Scott asked his friend, helping him across the ice.

Laura started up after them, hanging back a little, wondering what to do next.

"No, I'll stay. I'm good," Will insisted, brushing off the whole thing. "Just a little technical problem with my brakes, that's all!"

Scott laughed. "You've got to learn how to turn, man!"

"So show me."

Laura watched as Scott skated ahead.

"This is how you do it. I can't tell you exactly—I guess it has to do with leaning on one side of the blades and using the weight of your body. I never really thought about it."

No, but you can do it without thinking! Watching closely, Laura was sure that Scott was a natural skater. He had great flow and balance, almost as if he'd been born with ice skates on his feet. She allowed her hopes to rise again.

"So how do you stop?" novice Will asked.

Scott showed him and made him do it. "It's a little bit like skiing," he explained. "Have you ever skied?"

Will shook his head. "I play anything with a ball," he confessed, "but put me on a slippery surface, and I'm dead!

C'mon, I'm out of here. Let's go and get a cold drink."

Okay, this is it! Laura decided. *It's now or never!* She skated up to the two boys. "This might sound weird . . ." she began.

"No way!" was the first thing Scott said.

"You've got to be kidding!" Will said with a laugh.

"I mean it—I need a new partner!" Laura stood on the crowded ice, trying to make Scott believe that she was serious.

"I don't do ice dancing!" Scott told her. "Okay, so these are figure skates—I borrowed them from my dad. He used to do a few twirls on the ice. But not me. Now, if you'd said ice hockey, I might be interested. I played a lot last winter."

"Ice dancing!" Will echoed mockingly.

"Listen, my partner just got injured. Scott, I saw you skate hip-hop on the ice the other day, and I've been watching you again today—you're a good skater!"

Scott grimaced and then shrugged. "Yeah, I like it. But ice *dancing*?"

"What's wrong with that?" Laura wanted to know. "You'd better not diss it. You've got to be tough to get through all the training—especially the lifts."

"You don't get it," Will interrupted, speaking up for his friend. "Scott's thing is soccer. He plays with me on Manchester United's junior team."

"Yeah, that's cool," Laura went on. "My big brother is soccer-crazy too." She thought she'd spotted a glimmer of interest in Scott's eyes, in spite of what Will had said. "But this would only be four weeks out of your life. Y'know, like on TV—where they take someone who works in an office and turn them into an opera singer or something, and then they fool the professional judges!"

"Four weeks?" he repeated. "Then what?"

"Then we fly to Canada for the

international Junior Grand Prix in Montreal. Then back to school, and you can play all the soccer you want for the rest of your life!"

Now there was a definite light shining through the questions and doubts. "Montreal?" Scott murmured.

"Man, you're not taking this stuff seriously, are you?" Will scoffed, backing off and shaking his head. "You're Mr. Cool. You don't do ice dancing!"

"No way!" Scott toughed it out in front of Will. "I'm not even thinking of saying yes."

"Okay, cool," Will grunted, wobbling off on his skates to join the rest of the gang.

Scott narrowed his eyes and kept on looking at Laura. "Canada?" he checked again.

She nodded. Now that she had Scott on his own, she felt that she might be able to persuade him. "If you're good enough.

47

And if your parents agree." Laura felt that Scott's dad's ice-skating history might help here. She'd checked Scott's skates closely and saw that they were pretty well made, which meant that his dad had been a serious skater in his time.

"My dad will be cool," he told her, confirming her gut feeling. "My mum's not around anymore."

"Okay, so it comes down to whether you'll be good enough."

Scott thought a while longer. "Do I have to wear tights?"

She grinned. "No."

"Sequins?"

"Not if you don't want to." *Yes, he's weakening!* she thought.

"No sequins." Scott laid it on the line. "Who'll teach me? . . . If I say I'll do it!"

Laura took a deep breath. "Me to start with. Then there's my coach, Vera Mozer. She was an Olympic champion in the eighties. She's the best."

Scott nodded and thought it through. "I've seen you training with her," he confessed. "You're pretty good."

"Thanks. So?" She still held her breath, waiting for the answer.

"Okay, I'll do it!" Scott said. "When do we start?"

It was early Saturday morning. Only Laura and Scott were on the ice. Inside the empty rink, the music echoed.

"It's called a paso doble," Laura told Scott. "Listen to the beat. It's a bit tricky, but once you've got it in your head, you can take two steps and kick with your right leg, like this."

Scott yawned. "It's too early," he moaned. "I should be at home in bed!"

"Watch!" Laura skated the steps again. "Now you do it."

Her new partner shrugged and copied her perfectly.

"Cool." Laura was surprised by how

easily he did it. "Now add a back swing and a ninety-degree turn on your left leg, like this."

Scott watched carefully. "What are you doing with your arms?"

"Pretending to be a bullfighter waving his cape. You have to get into the spirit of the dance."

"Man!" Scott groaned, reluctantly copying Laura's arm movements.

"Stop whining. After the quarter turn, we link arms and take five steps on the diagonal, and then you have to lift me."

"Hey, slow down!" Scott struggled to follow. "This lift—do we have to try it right now?"

Laura shook her head. "Do I look stupid? No way would I trust you with the lifts until we've worked them out in the gym."

"Who said anything about the gym?"

"I did. Tonight, after your soccer game."

Scott made the face of a kid who's just

been told he has detention. "Do I have to?"

Laura laughed and nodded. "No pain, no gain," she told him. "Think Canada. Think Montreal. Now, c'mon, try this diagonal sequence again!"

"I hate hospitals," Patrick admitted when Laura visited him that afternoon.

He was in a bed with a cage over his broken leg, propped up on pillows and looking pale and bored.

She'd brought some grapes, which they ate together.

"How have your mum and dad taken it?" Laura asked, fidgeting in her seat.

Patrick wrinkled his nose. "Y'know . . ."

"Yeah, I can guess." His parents were probably giving him a hard time without meaning to. They wouldn't be able to hide their disappointment about him missing Montreal. "Does your leg hurt?"

He nodded. "Why did this have to happen?"

"I know—it's terrible." Laura wondered about mentioning Scott and then decided against it. After all, Patrick had enough on his plate. "I hate hospitals too," she confessed, staring out the window at the rows of cars parked below.

"Hey, I don't weigh that much!" Laura cried as Scott tried the lift, mistimed it, and failed. His legs buckled, and they both collapsed on the floor.

It was Saturday evening. They had met in the gym down the road from Laura's house. Scott was dressed in sweatpants and his usual cool T-shirt; Laura wore a leotard under her sweatshirt.

"Show me again," Scott said. "Hang on. You take three steps toward me, I bend my knee, you step up, and I use your forward motion to lift you onto my shoulder, and you do your dying-swan thing. Is that it?"

"Forget the dying swan. This has to be upbeat, loads of energy. Are you ready?"

Taking a deep breath, Scott nodded.

"Promise not to drop me?" she asked. "I don't want to go shooting straight over your shoulder and fall on my face!"

He nodded again, his face tense. He bent one knee in preparation. "Go ahead!"

Laura ran and stepped neatly onto Scott's knee. He put both hands on her waist and lifted her onto his shoulder, where she balanced, one leg bent, the other fully extended. She threw back her head and spread her arms out like a bird in flight. "Okay, now put me down!"

Scott wobbled and almost overbalanced. Laura collapsed over his shoulder like a sack of potatoes. He staggered and let her slither to the floor. "You never told me how to put you down!" he gasped.

"Oops!" Laura rolled away and then sprang to her feet, tugging on her ponytail and straightening her top. The session wasn't going too badly, considering. They were both working hard to get things right.

"Hey, how did your soccer game go?" she asked, waiting for him to recover his balance.

"We won, two-zero." Scott was in a good mood, grinning at the fiasco of the failed lift.

"Cool," Laura said and smiled back. "Now maybe we can try this move one more time!"

Chapter 5

"How come you're so good at sports?" Laura asked Scott while they took a break from the ice during a practice session the following morning.

She wiped the moisture off her skates as they sat in the café overlooking the busy rink. Scott was due to leave at noon to get to afternoon soccer practice on time. "You've got to be good at something," he said and shrugged. "And I tell you one thing, I'm not winning any science or math prizes, and according to my English teacher, there's no way I will ever write a bestseller!"

"You don't care, do you?" Laura had already picked up that he was totally laid-back. Nothing seemed to bother him.

"Nope. It drives my dad crazy. He thinks that I should work harder. All in all, Dad's cool, though. He comes to watch me play soccer every Saturday—he hasn't missed a game in two years!"

"And is he okay about you doing this training with me?" Laura wanted to know.

Scott nodded. "He says I'm living the life he always dreamed of for himself. His attitude is 'Go for it!'"

"That's fantastic. It's my mum more than my dad who's into the skating stuff." Laura took a sip of her drink, wiggling her ankles and flexing her shoulders so that she didn't stiffen up. "She's the one who drives me to the competitions. But they're both pretty easygoing, actually." Not like Patrick's parents, who never stopped pushing him.

Scott nodded, biting into a Mars bar and aiming the wrapper at the closest trash can. He scored a direct hit. "So, what keeps you going? I mean, you're telling me we have to be up before dawn every single day if we want to get ready for this competition. That's a whole month of not enough sleep for me, but you must have been doing that forever!"

"Since I was eight," she admitted. She thought for a while. "I suppose I keep going because I just love it!"

"But love *what* exactly?"

"I don't know. What do you love about soccer?"

"Hey, I just mess around. I can kick a ball better than the next kid, I guess."

Laura shook her head. "I don't believe that. I think, deep down, you love the game. Like, I'm totally happy when I'm on the ice, like I'm flying or soaring. I love every second."

Scott grinned. "Maybe."

"Yes!" she insisted. "You're scared to say it, but you LOVE soccer! You work hard at it, you put in every bit of energy to play well—I could tell you do when you said that you won two–zero."

He got up and walked toward the metal stairs. "Maybe," he called over his shoulder. "But don't ever tell anyone I said that!"

"Wow, look at Scott!" The cry went up when he and Laura took to the ice to practice their paso doble. "Hey, that's not hip-hop—what is it?"

"We've got to get our leg swings exactly together," Laura insisted, ignoring the remarks. "And when I turn away from you to go into my spin, you have to skate backward and then curve around to meet me."

"Just watch—I'll crash into someone," Scott warned, glancing over his shoulder.

"Stay out of his way," a kid said, clearing the space for him and Laura.

"Ready?" Scott checked.

She nodded, counting out the beat of the music. One, two, three. Off they went, stepping across the ice, high kicking and then turning in opposite directions. Laura gathered her arms to spin. Scott sped backward and then curved around to join her.

"Did you see that?" a friend of Scott's called out. "Their feet went up higher than their heads. Whoa, baby!"

"Good!" Laura nodded, catching Scott's hand and skating on. "Now let's try the lift."

He looked doubtfully at her. So far, though they'd worked it out at the gym, they hadn't tried it on the ice. "You sure?"

Laura knew that this was no time to stop, think, and get scared. "Yeah, let's try."

"Three steps, and then you bend your right leg toward your chest. I catch you by the waist and raise you to my shoulder."

"You've got it."

"Okay, let's do it."

Skating apart, knowing that all eyes were on them, Scott and Laura prepared for the lift. "One, two, three!" She tapped her hip to set up the tempo and then set off across the ice. *Skate fast, hope that he grabs ahold of me, use the speed, soar through the air. . . .*

There was a look of panic on Scott's face as Laura sped toward him. Then he locked into her rhythm and timing, caught hold of her, and hoisted her up onto his shoulder. "We did it!" he muttered, sailing on across the ice.

"Did you see it?" the watching kids gasped. "How cool was that?"

There was a wave of excitement; a few people clapped.

Scott skated on, lowering Laura to the ground, and then breathed a sigh of relief. "Are you okay?" he asked.

She nodded, a grin splitting her face from ear to ear. "Cool!" she said. "It felt good. I knew you could do it."

"Yeah, go, Scott!" some other kids cheered.

There was only one person there who

didn't look happy, and that was Will, sitting in the café with another soccer pal, looking down at Scott and Laura's antics on the ice. "What's he doing?" he muttered. "Scott told me that he wasn't going to do this. It's not right."

"How come?" Charlie asked. "It looked okay to me."

Will shook his head. "It's not okay, dummy. It's scary stuff."

Charlie disagreed. "What's scary about dancing?"

"At fifty miles an hour, wearing a pair of knife-sharp blades on your feet!" Will retorted. "If they had an accident, Scott could really hurt himself."

The two boys watched as Laura took their friend to one side and coached him, ready for the next lift. Then Will got up. "I'm out of here," he told Charlie. "If Scott Yorke wants to wreck his chances of a career in professional soccer, why should I care?"

Chapter 6

"Laura, I'm confused." Helen Lee came up to Laura's room later that night. "I just picked up a phone message from Vera saying that she can meet you at seven tomorrow morning."

"Good." Laura ducked her head half under the covers and tried to sound sleepy.

"But why did you ask her to do that?" Laura's mum hadn't expected to be on taxi duty now that Patrick was injured. "What's the point of carrying on training without your partner?"

Laura disappeared further from sight. She didn't want to tell anyone about Scott until after Vera had seen him and said he was good enough to be Laura's partner. It would be like jinxing their chances. "Mum, I'm tired!"

"So you want me to drive you in?"

"Please, if you don't mind."

"And you don't think you should take it easy—do something else for a change, allow yourself to get over the disappointment of Montreal?"

Yawn, turn over, sound half asleep. "No, I want to keep on training."

Helen nodded. "Okay," she agreed, closing the door softly behind her.

"I'm a bit worried about Laura," she confessed to her husband when she went downstairs. "She's all revved up and on edge. I don't think she's taking Patrick's accident well at all."

The next day, Laura was the first to arrive at the rink.

"I'll stay and watch if you want," her mum offered, handing Laura her sports bag from the back of the car.

"No, thanks!" Laura hurried off toward the entrance with its unlit neon sign and scattering of loose tickets littering the ground. Her plan was to meet with Vera and talk to her before Scott showed up.

He'll probably be late, she thought anxiously. *Scott's not the type to get here on time!*

So she hung around at the entrance, looking out for her coach's familiar fur hat and bright pink padded jacket, which she wore all year-round.

The coach soon pulled up in her red car, stepping out and striding toward the entrance, surprised to see Laura lurking there. "Why aren't you changed and ready to warm up?" she asked.

"I wanted to explain something before we start." Walking through the entrance, Laura felt her pulse start to race. What she was about to say didn't sound convincing, even to her.

Vera shrugged. "Darling, it's okay if

you want to keep on training without Patrick. I admire your dedication—it's how champions are made."

"No, that's not what I meant. . . ."

"There's plenty of work you can do on your own. We can improve your footwork without him."

"No, Vera—listen!" Laura jogged to keep up with her coach's long stride. She'd heard the door open behind them and guessed that Scott had just arrived. "I want to tell you something."

"Hey, Laura!" Scott called. "Sorry I'm late."

Vera turned with a puzzled expression. Then she faced Laura.

Laura grimaced. *This isn't how it was meant to happen. I was supposed to set things up and convince her before Scott got here.* But here they were, Scott and Vera, face-to-face. "Vera, this is Scott Yorke. Scott, meet Vera Mozer!"

★ ★ ★

"Just run that by me again!" the coach said in disbelief.

Scott, Laura, and Vera stood by the side of the rink, under the glaring lights.

Vera held up a well-manicured hand. "No, forget that. Let me repeat what I think I just heard you say! Laura, you want Scott to be your new partner? Scott, you want me to work with you on our routines and get you ready in time for Montreal?"

Laura nodded. She kept her fingers firmly crossed behind her back. "I know it's a bit unexpected," she murmured.

"Darling, do you want to give me a heart attack?" Vera looked Scott up and down and then turned back to Laura. "It's impossible!"

"Okay, no worries—I'm out of here." Scott shrugged, readily doing an about-face. No way did he like the look of Vera Mozer, who looked even tougher than his soccer coach.

Laura panicked. "No, wait! Listen, Vera, you haven't seen Scott skate. He's really good!"

"He could be a genius for all I care." Vera shook her head and put up both hands in protest. "It's a crazy idea, Laura. We only have four weeks. No way is it going to work."

"Yeah, it's crazy," Scott agreed, taking the easy way out and setting off for the exit.

Laura ran after him and then darted back to Vera. "You're not even giving me a chance!" she cried. "We've been working together all weekend. At least take a look at what we can do!"

Vera frowned, glancing toward Scott's rapidly disappearing figure. Then she looked hard at Laura, seeing the determination that she knew so well. "You're serious, aren't you?"

"Completely. He's good, Vera. He's played ice hockey. He learns fast."

"He has a good physique," the coach

admitted. "Tall and strong for his age. A natural athlete."

Ignoring their discussion, Scott swung through the door and left the building.

"Please!" Laura begged. This meant more to her than anything in her entire life.

Vera tilted her head back and slowly brought it forward again. "Go bring him back," she agreed. "Let's see what he can do."

"Don't be nervous, okay!" Laura stood with Scott in the center of the rink. She'd had to work hard to persuade him to come back and face Vera.

"What's there to be nervous about?" he said with a self-mocking grin. "I'm only about to make an idiot of myself!"

"Paso doble—remember the rhythm, keep in time to the music, do all the arm stuff like I showed you." Laura waited for Vera to play the music, and her heart was in her throat.

"Yeah," Scott muttered. He still wasn't

sure about Scary Woman in her fur hat.

The notes started, and they went smoothly into the routine, keeping perfect time and synchronizing every step. Together they swung their legs and turned, spun, and then Scott went down on one knee to continue the spin, while Laura kicked her leg high up over his head.

"Hmm!" Vera said from the side of the ice rink.

Now they were up, hands linked and gliding on. It was time for the step sequence, followed by the lift.

"Ready?" Laura asked under her breath.

"This is fun!" Scott grinned back. The steps went perfectly, and then he split off from her in a wide curve.

Three steps and up, flying through the air, soaring along in a perfect lift!

Scott carried Laura close to where Vera stood and then lowered her down to the ice. They skated the final steps together.

"So?" Laura and Scott said.

The coach couldn't disguise her amazement. Her eyes were wide, and her mouth hung open as she stared from Laura to Scott. Then she blinked and stared again.

"What do you think?" Laura prompted.

Vera cleared her throat, shaking her head as if trying to dismiss what she'd just seen. "I don't believe it," she said.

"Well—do I stay or do I go?" Scott asked, seeing the funny side, as always.

"Don't joke," Vera told him. "Ice dancing is serious. Laura has pinned her hopes on you."

"Sorry." He lowered his head to hide the triumph that he still felt.

"Can we do it?" Laura asked. "Do you think we can get Scott ready for Montreal?"

Laura's coach spread her hands and raised her eyebrows before she gave her verdict. "We can try," she said at last.

Chapter 7

"No one said it would be easy," Laura reminded Scott.

They were four days into their official training with Vera, spending every minute that they could on the ice. Their muscles ached; their bodies were bruised and battered. Now they sat together in the café, huddled over hot chocolate and cake.

"Yeah, but no one said it would be this hard either." Two days earlier, Scott had brought his dad to meet Vera, and they'd made the arrangements to get him measured and fitted with his own top-class skates. Now he was wearing them, and they were giving him blisters.

"Harder than soccer practice?" she asked.

"Different. At soccer practice you're part of a team, having a laugh. With Vera, every second is deadly serious."

Today, for instance, she had pulled Scott up a thousand times—"More lift and extension on the left leg. . . . Watch your posture. . . . Control your feet!"

"Don't let Vera get to you," Laura said, picking up on what he was thinking. "I know she seems really strict, but she's a cool teacher."

"She's a slave driver," he complained. "I reckon she never says anything nice, even if you're dying out there."

Taking a big bite of cake, unable to deny what he'd just said, Laura sat and thought for a while about how she could help Scott through this first week. They were starting by learning the compulsory paso doble before they moved on to the original program of salsa and rumba. "Look at it this way," she told him. "If you can survive four weeks of Vera, you get to go to Canada."

"Hey, maybe I'll get to see some ice hockey!" Scott's eyes lit up. "Cool!"

"Plus, we're there with a chance of a medal, remember!" Okay, so there was a mountain of work that was as steep as a ski slope still to get through, but Laura hadn't given up hope of the bronze medal at least.

Unluckily for her, their conversation was interrupted by the arrival of Will, Charlie, and a bunch more of Scott's friends. They crowded around, demanding to know how the routines were going.

"Hey, Scott, how are the pirouettes coming?" Will asked, enjoying putting his friend under pressure. He hadn't forgiven Scott for lying to him about not doing the wimpy ice-dancing stuff. "Did you get your ballet costume sorted out yet?"

Scott sniffed and sat with a blank expression.

"Come on—what color are your tights?" Will joked. He was a tough-looking kid with scruffy, mouse-brown hair and a top lip that lifted readily into a scoffing grin.

"We don't do pirouettes, and boys don't wear tights for ice dancing!" Laura said, setting Will straight. "Listen, give us a break, will you?"

"Tip-tip-tip, tippety-toe!" Will jeered, miming a ballet dancer and making everyone laugh.

On top of the bruises and recent falls, this was more than Scott could take. "Jeez!" he said, scraping back his chair and walking away. He disappeared into the bathroom, to the sound of his friends' laughter.

Laura frowned and glared at Will, who sat down across from her. "Thanks!"

Will pushed out his bottom lip and shrugged. "Don't mention it."

"I keep telling you—this isn't funny. Anyway, what's wrong with Scott going to Canada? Why are you trying to spoil it for him?"

At first Will denied it, but as Scott

reappeared and toughed it out with his other friends, Will suddenly got serious with Laura. "Think about it," he said, leaning across the table toward her. "Tell me what happened with your first partner—Patrick what's-his-name. He had an accident, didn't he?"

Laura narrowed her eyes and nodded. She could already see where this was leading.

"I hear he broke his kneecap." Will leaned back in his chair, slowly shaking his head. "What if that happens to Scott? Where does that leave him?"

"I don't know—you tell me."

"It leaves him with no contract for United Juniors, which is what he's aiming for at the start of next season! If he breaks a leg, he's finished!"

Laura took a deep breath and then sighed. She stood up and walked away. "He won't break his leg!" she muttered. "He'll win a medal—you'll see!"

★ ★ ★

"Keep a clean line, Scott. No, that's not good enough. Try again!" Vera picked at him over and over again, through the weekend and into the early part of the following week.

Laura demonstrated the moves, aware that her mum was standing beside Vera, keeping a close eye on what was going on.

"Can you show me that again?" Scott asked Laura.

She went into a combination spin, stopped, and got Scott to copy her.

"I don't get it," he muttered, coming out of it and shaking his head.

"Watch—it's easy." Again she did the move and then watched him copy her. Scott wobbled and looked dizzy as he came to a halt.

"We haven't got all day!" Vera shouted across the ice. Impatient though she was at the best of times, working with Scott seemed to be making her temper even worse.

Laura noticed her mum lean over and speak to the coach. "Yeah, tell her to give us a break!" she muttered under her breath. She nodded as Scott rehearsed the spin again and finally got it. "The salsa has to have lots of fast spins," she explained. "But once you've gotten used to the speed, it all comes pretty smoothly."

"Says you!" Today there was no joking, no fun in it as far as he was concerned. "Doesn't Scary Woman ever let up?"

Laura shook her head. "But, underneath, she's cool. She cares."

"Yeah, about reliving her glory days by getting us to win another gold medal for her," Scott grumbled, deep in the doldrums. "I reckon it's not actually us that she cares about."

Laura skated backward, circling around while Vera decided what they should do next. She frowned as she thought about what Scott had just said, and then she came back to join him. "That's not true," she decided. "I know Vera seems strict, but . . ."

"Heart of ice. Ice queen!" Scott insisted, glancing at the two women by the barrier.

". . . but, no, underneath she's kind. I've seen it. I know she is!"

Laura's serious expression brought the old smile back to Scott's face. "I believe you!" he said with a grin. "Like, yeah, I really do!"

The second week of training did not get easier as it went on. For a start, Scott and Laura had taken more falls than usual. Their skates had clicked together during a step sequence and brought them down, sending them skidding across the ice on their backs. Then Scott had lost control of the combination spin in the salsa and ended up pulling Laura down. And so it went on.

Besides, Vera's mood had worsened. By the end of the week, she was so gloomy that even Laura was beginning to think that her idea of finding a new partner had been a mistake.

And now, at 10:30 on Friday evening, as Scott and Laura collapsed, exhausted, on the bench at the side of the rink, Laura's phone rang, and she saw Patrick's name come up on the tiny screen.

"Hi, Patrick!" she said, trying to sound more cheerful than she felt. "How are you?"

Scott leaned back against the row of chairs behind him, legs stretched out, arms hanging by his sides.

". . .Yeah, I'm fine, thanks." Quickly, Laura picked up a note of worry in Patrick's voice. ". . . I'm at the ice rink. Why do you ask?"

"Okay, Scott, that's enough for today," Vera was telling him. "Go home to bed."

Laura listened to the voice on the phone for a while and then spoke again. ". . .Yeah, actually, that's true. How did you find out? . . . No, I wasn't trying to hide it from you. . . . No, don't worry. Yeah, I would have told you soon. . . ."

"What's up?" Scott asked, glad to be left alone by Vera, who had walked off to speak to Laura's mum.

". . . Honestly, Patrick, I'm not going behind your back. And whatever your dad's told you, this isn't a permanent thing. No . . . yes. I'm sorry. Bye." She sighed and sagged forward as she ended the call.

"So, that was Patrick!" Scott groaned. Every time he moved, a new muscle ached. "Sounds to me like you're in trouble."

"I should have been up-front before now and told him that I was working with a new partner," Laura said and sighed again. "Only I was waiting for the right moment, and now his dad has somehow found out and broken the news to him out of the blue."

"Yeah, I guessed." By now, Scott was sitting up and paying attention. "So Patrick's not happy?"

Laura shook her head. She felt terrible about the phone conversation that she'd just had.

There was a long silence, with Laura and Scott both staring out across the empty rink, before Scott spoke again. "You know what?" he said. "I'm thinking this might not be such a great idea after all."

Laura's heart jumped, but she tried to hold her voice steady. "Hey, come on," she coaxed. "I'll visit Patrick and put him in the picture. He won't mind in the end."

"It's not just that. There's all this work, and I haven't finished learning the original section yet. We haven't even started on the free dance."

"We have over two weeks left. You can do it!" Laura felt her stomach churn. She was afraid that Scott was on the point of walking away.

"Then there's Scary Woman," he muttered. "It's no fun when you've got her on your back, day in and day out!"

"I don't think it's Patrick or the work or Vera," Laura challenged. "I think what's really bugging you is Will!"

"That's stupid!" Scott stood up and got his skates. He was annoyed with Laura because she'd seen through his excuses and hit the nail on the head. No way did he want his friends laughing and making fun of him. "Anyway, whatever. I'm out of here!"

Laura joined her mum, feeling as though her world had ended. Scott had walked out on her. She had no partner for Montreal.

Helen Lee took one look at her daughter and marched her straight out to the car. "No need to talk," she said. "Let me guess—Scott has changed his mind?"

Miserably, Laura nodded. "In a way, I don't blame him."

"Shh." Her mum steered the car out of the lot. "I knew Vera was putting too much pressure on him. I had a word with her about it earlier this week."

"I know, Mum. Thanks. But it wasn't just that. I mean, Scott's a laid-back guy who just wants to have fun. But he can work hard too, and he was getting really good."

"So what made him change his mind?" Stopped in traffic, Helen glanced at Laura and spotted weary tears trickling down her cheeks.

"Stupid stuff!" Laura said and sniffed. "Partly 'cause Patrick found out what was happening and had a tantrum."

"Which can be fixed," Helen pointed out. "We just have to explain that Scott is only your partner while Patrick is out of action. Then it'll be back to the old partnership with you and Patrick—won't it?"

Laura nodded. "Scott wants to play soccer for United. That's really his thing. I'll want to skate with Patrick again, once he's feeling better."

"So, no problem." Helen insisted on a positive way of seeing things. "What else?"

Laura got to the nitty-gritty. "Scott's soccer buddies are making fun of him. He can't take it."

"Now that really is silly!" Laura's mum eased through the lights and made a quick turn to the left. She pulled into a supermarket parking lot. "Ice dancing is a tough discipline. It's not for wimps!"

"I know that, but stupid Will doesn't!"

Helen thought for a while. "It seems to me that there's nothing here that can't be fixed, Laura. Listen to me—this is what we're going to do!"

Chapter 8

While Laura's mum went to see Mr. and Mrs. Cole to explain the real situation, Laura sat at home and sent a text message to Scott: *Need 2 c u now*

She waited five minutes for a reply and then sent a second message: *Ansa me!!!*

One more minute, and then a reply arrived. *Nothing 2 say. Bye!*

Still need 2 c u!

Go away—end of story

"Says who?" Laura muttered, switching to more direct action. She punched in Scott's number and waited for him to answer.

"Don't you get it, Laura? Leave me alone!" He answered the call and came straight at her. "I'm up to here with double twists and triple throw loops. I never want to hear another salsa as long as I live!"

"Tell me where you live. I need to talk to you."

Scott didn't believe what he was hearing. "Are you deaf? Or just crazy?"

Laura laughed. "Crazy, I guess! You have to be, to do what I do!"

"I knew it!" Scott laughed back. "I'm dealing with Crazy Girl."

"And Scary Woman," she reminded him. "Listen, I have an idea. No one knows about it yet—not even Vera. But I need to see you face-to-face. Come on, tell me—where do you live?"

There was a long pause. "If I see you now, do you promise not to stalk me for the rest of my life?"

"Yeah, promise!"

"And just for five minutes, okay?"

"Five minutes." She grinned as Scott

gave her the address. "Cool. That's only ten minutes from here on foot. Wait there. Bye!"

"Five minutes, then adios." Scott opened the door warily to let Laura in. He was still in his sweatpants but had thrown on the old United shirt that he wore around the house. "So what's new?"

Laura breezed into the hallway. "Mum's gone around to the Coles' place to calm them down. I've come here to talk about our free dance section."

"*Our* free dance section?" he echoed. "There is no 'our,' remember?"

"But there will be after you've listened to this," she went on. "Okay, so it's risky and no one's ever done anything like this before, but once the judges get their heads around it, they'll see it's really cool, and if we get it right, they'll give it top scores— you've got to believe me!"

"Whoa, whoa, whoa!" Scott backed off

against a table. "What are you talking about, Crazy Girl?"

"*Our* free dance," she insisted. "The third component—it's the part where we get to do our own thing to one long piece of music—you know, the dying-swan bit."

Scott shook his head wearily. "I don't know where this is going," he groaned, "but just spit it out, will you?"

"Okay." Laura's eyes sparkled. She'd gotten back all of her energy and enthusiasm. "The couples who will be skating in Montreal—they'll all be dancing to waltz music or sambas or cha-chas—stuff that everybody expects. But it came to me in a flash—why don't we do something completely different— something modern and funky that nobody has ever done before!"

"Like what?" Scott asked and frowned, still trying to guess what was coming.

"You'll like it!" she promised. "At first I thought jitterbug or rock and roll—you know, real fifties stuff. But other ice-dancing couples already do that. Then I thought, why not get even more modern—why not street music, why not hip-hop?"

"Now you're seriously crazy," Scott muttered, showing her the door.

"Wait! Hip-hop with really cool, loud music that *you* can choose. And you'll have to teach me the moves over the next couple of days, and next week Vera will make it fit the Grand Prix requirements, with all the lifts and spins and stuff thrown in. . . ."

"Hmm!" Scott started to give Laura's idea some serious thought. "Would it be allowed?" he double-checked.

She nodded eagerly. "Think about it—if we dance hip-hop, none of your friends will be able to make fun of us. In fact, even Will would think it's cool."

"I'm already cool," Scott reminded her. "Or I was—until you came along!"

"Okay, I'll be cool too. C'mon, Scott,

hip-hop, street rhythms, funky music!"

"Huh!" he said, looking at Laura as if she was a little less crazy than he'd thought. He pictured them both on the ice, mirroring each other's moves, getting into the spirit of hip-hop and break dancing. "You know, that just might work!"

Laura felt relief spread over her like a warm shower. Her face relaxed into a bright smile. "So, will you?" she asked.

Scott nodded. "I guess Crazy Girl talked me into it," he said.

The next morning at the ice rink during the public session, Laura explained to Scott that they didn't want to hit their coach full in the face with their hip-hop idea. "Music wise, Vera's stuck in the seventies and eighties," she told him. "If we said we were doing Abba, she'd be fine."

They both broke into a version of "Dancing Queen," sang a few bars, and then burst out laughing.

Other kids around the rink took up the song and began to do 80s dance moves on the ice.

"We have to go behind her back and work on some moves today," Laura went on. "But I'm relying on you. I don't have a clue how to begin."

Scott grinned and told her to switch on the track. He had brought in an iPod loaded with the song that he'd chosen and some speakers.

"For a start, we've got to get the rhythm." He started moving to the fast, strong beat with broken rhythms and scratch sounds, attracting a small crowd, including Laura's friend Abi and Scott's friend—and Laura's major enemy—Will.

Laura copied Scott, and soon some of the others joined in, but when Scott dropped low and went into a spin on one leg, only Laura followed. Abi tried it but quickly overbalanced and fell. "The beat is too fast!" she cried, picking herself up.

Coming out of the spin, Scott leaned forward into a handstand.

"Uh-oh, no!" Laura ground to a halt, hands on her hips. "Ice-dancing rules won't let us put our hands on the ice."

Scott stopped and thought again. "What about a step sequence like this?"

Once more he demonstrated, and Laura copied. "Cool!" she said, a big smile spreading over her face. They strung together the opening arm movements, the spin, and the steps.

"Hip-hop!" Abi grinned and clapped. "Is this for your program in Montreal?"

Laura nodded. "Top secret. Don't tell anyone!"

"Fat chance," Will muttered. "There's only twenty people standing here watching!"

She ignored him. "We can spin on our knees, do high kicks, I can slide between your legs, you can swing your leg over my head, anything except touching the ice with our hands."

"And we need a few lifts?" Scott checked.

She nodded. "Some straight, some rotational. The harder the better, 'cause we score higher for degree of difficulty. But for now, I think we have to get the opening sequence right so that we can show Vera what we've been working on."

For a few minutes they rehearsed the moves, getting them smoother and more synchronized. Laura loved the fast, funky rhythm and threw herself into the flowing hip-hop style, following Scott's every move.

"That looks great!" Abi encouraged, and even Will stopped scowling and added a suggestion or two of his own.

"Hey, throw in a dance off. Scott, you do your thing and then challenge Laura to do one better. Y'know, break-dance stuff!"

"Cool!" Gradually, Scott and Laura were clearing a bigger space on the ice and attracting more kids. Everyone was clapping as the pair took up Will's idea and tried to outdance each other.

Laura watched Scott do a diagonal step sequence with a couple of turns and a low, crouching spin. She took him on with a slow, funky series of turning steps, ending in a double twist.

"Go, Laura!" the girls cried.

"Go, Scott!" the boys replied.

Grinning and laughing, they danced themselves to a standstill, while the little kids took over the ice and tried to copy the simpler moves.

"What do you think?" Scott asked Will as they headed for the barrier to take a break. He really wanted to get his friend back on his side.

There was a long pause. Will went through his own struggle with pride and resentment and his serious worries that Scott could get injured. "I think bling," he said in the end.

"Meaning?"

"Meaning, forget the sequins—go for bling."

"Are you talking about our costumes?" Laura asked.

The tough soccer star of tomorrow nodded. "Big gold chains, bro. Plenty of chest on show."

"Does that mean you think it's cool now?" Scott asked, grinning at Laura behind his friend's back.

Will grunted and then nodded. "Go for it, dude. Go to Montreal. This stuff will knock 'em senseless!"

Laura felt like she'd climbed a high mountain during these last two-and-a-half weeks and was nearing the top. The summit was in sight.

Okay, she'd hit a few obstacles—a sheer rock face that looked unclimbable, the unsuspected crevasse and occasional avalanche that had sent her sliding into the depths. But now, with Scott back on board and everyone at the rink telling them that the hip-hop program was a fantastic idea, her hopes were high.

"Well done, Laura. I'm pleased for you," her mum told her that night, coming into her room to tell her that it was time for lights out. "You've shown real guts to get this far after Patrick had his accident."

"The main thing was persuading Scott to stick with it," Laura explained. For once she was ready to go to sleep, her body exhausted after her day at the rink. "But now we've got this really cool program for the free dance, which we're going to show Vera tomorrow."

Helen nodded. "Like I said, you've given it everything you've got. So what's the new program? Is it going to be a waltz or something a bit more up-tempo?"

"Up-tempo," Laura said with a smile, deliberately keeping it secret until after she and Scott had shown Vera their ideas.

"Laura, what aren't you telling me?"

"Surprise!" Laura laughed and snuggled under the covers. "Wait until tomorrow morning, and then you'll see!"

Chapter 9

"I've altered the details on the plane tickets for Montreal," Vera told Scott first thing the following morning. "I've given the airline your name instead of Patrick's. Everything's fine."

They'd met, as usual, at a time when the rink was opened especially for them. Vera was dressed, as always, in her fur hat and pink padded jacket; Scott and Laura were in their practice gear. Scott had brought in his hip-hop CD, which he had tucked away underneath the CD player on Vera's folding rink-side table.

"Anyway, no time to stand and chat," Vera said briskly. "Scott, did you get your blades sharpened, like I told you?"

He nodded, feeling more nervous than usual.

"Did you warm up, both of you?" the coach asked.

"Before you got here," Laura said.

"So, we begin to think today about our free program," Vera went on. "Scott, I want to teach you the same program we had for Patrick. Laura knows it already, which means that she can help you learn."

Laura wrinkled her nose and twitched her mouth to one side. "Um . . ."

"It's a very classical piece," Vera went on. "Everything must flow to a waltz time. It requires grace and control."

"Actually . . ." Laura interrupted. She was trying to figure out how to explain. *Don't hit her in the face with it,* she reminded herself. *Break it to her gently.*

But Scott charged like a bull in a china shop. "Watch this!" he told Vera, sliding the CD into the player before grabbing Laura by the hand and skating into the center of the ice.

Vera stood by the side of the ice, her mouth wrinkled like a prune, wondering what was going on.

The break-dance music shattered the silence of the vast space with an explosion of drumbeats and scratchy keyboard sounds. Scott and Laura took up the broken rhythms and went into their opening sequence.

"Forget classical!" Scott muttered. "Try hip-hop instead!"

"My God!" Vera cried, putting her hands on her ears. "What is this?"

Rushed into their dance without preparation, Laura had to throw caution to the wind. *Okay, this is it!* she told herself. *Vera is either gonna love it or hate it!*

She and Scott snaked their hips and strutted, spun, and stepped until their coach suddenly stopped the music.

"What is this dreadful noise?" Vera demanded, turning to Helen Lee, who had just come in. "What is Laura thinking?"

Laura's mum shook her head. "It's news to me."

Laura took a deep breath and gritted her teeth. "I knew it. We should've broken it to her more gently!"

But Scott skated across to where the two women stood. "It's street music—break dance, hip-hop—all the kids are listening to it!"

"I don't care. It's disgusting!" Vera insisted, making a face as if she'd just swallowed live maggots. "What is wrong with a classical waltz or quickstep?"

"They're for old people," Scott told her, while Laura winced. "And we're not old—we're young. This is a *junior* championship, remember."

"Laura, what are you thinking?" Vera cried. "Have you forgotten everything I've taught you?"

At last, Laura found her voice. "You have to give us a chance," she insisted. "At least watch us again. Let us go through to the end of the sequence."

"That's fair enough," Helen agreed. "Let's not write it off without thinking about it some more."

Vera tutted and frowned. "I never heard anything like this music. It sounds like mice scratching around inside a tin drum!"

"But just watch this!" Eagerly, Laura skated ahead of Scott onto the ice and took up her starting position. This time she was ready to throw herself into the routine.

It was her mum who restarted the track.

Once more the hip-hop rhythms broke the silence. Scott went into the dance-off section with a stunning spin and then down into a split. Laura came back with a double lutz and then joined hands with Scott, and they set off at high speed on a diagonal sequence ending in a combination spin.

"Wow!" Helen Lee was taken aback. "That is actually pretty spectacular," she murmured.

The two women watched eagerly, taking in every step and turn. When the music ended, Vera sighed and beckoned the skaters to her.

"So?" Laura gasped. She knew that they'd danced well, but had they convinced their coach?

"Very original," Vera said, a deep frown line forming between her eyebrows. "But ugly."

"No!" Laura protested. "This is what kids like to dance to."

"We do," Scott agreed, looking from Vera to Helen and then back again.

"Ugly . . . but clever," Vera added, obviously thinking deeply. "And very, very risky."

"That's what we want to do—we want to take a risk!" Laura pleaded. "I've got a new partner. I'd like to do something that no one's ever done before!"

"Hmm." Still, the coach turned it over in her mind. "What about the judges? Are they ready? You know it could be a disaster in their eyes."

Slowly, Laura breathed out and then in again. "It's athletic. It looks fantastic—doesn't it, Mum?"

Helen backed off from the group. "Not my decision," she said quietly.

"Athletic—yes," Vera agreed. "It's a style that's suited to show off what the boy in the partnership can do, as well as the girl. And we could work in some sensational lifts. . . ."

"Say yes," Laura begged. This was the last big obstacle. If Vera refused, she didn't know what she would do.

Vera closed her eyes, opened them again, and nodded. "We will set the world of ice dancing on fire!" she agreed. "We will do something brand-new."

"Oh, fantastic!" Laura clasped her hands tightly together. Her eyes sparkled. "Oh, Vera, thank you!"

"But!" Their coach held up a warning finger. "Laura and Scott, if we are to win, you must work harder than you have ever worked before!"

Work, work, work—every waking minute of the week and a half before the Montreal championship, Laura lived and dreamed ice dancing.

She and Scott learned lifts from Vera that they had never even thought of—one in particular where they would skate back-to-back, elbows linked, and then Scott would lean forward and Laura would roll onto his back. Then she would swing both legs to her right and roll underneath him while he stood up straight and went into a spin. She had to hook her hands behind his neck and use their speed to fling her legs out behind her. All of this at high speed, so Laura was aware at times of her face dipping so close to the ice that her cheeks were sprinkled with the white powder rising from Scott's sharp blades.

"Ooh!" The onlookers gasped and

breathed a sigh of relief when Laura landed safely.

Meanwhile, Helen talked to Scott and Laura about costumes for the free dance.

"Will said bling," Laura reminded him. "But we can't wear chunky gold chains— they'd swing all over the place and be dangerous."

"We can have gold fabric medallion shapes sewn onto the tops," Helen suggested. "Laura, do you want to wear a skirt or pants?"

"Pants!" Her answer was instant. "Black. And a black half shirt with a logo. We need our costumes to look like a version of what hip-hop kids wear, not all floaty chiffon and frills."

"How about baseball caps?" Scott asked.

Vera groaned and walked away. "What was I thinking of, saying yes to this?" she muttered.

"Maybe not the caps?" Helen suggested tactfully.

"No caps," Laura agreed. Better not to push it too hard. After all, dear old Vera had already come a long way.

Work and sleep. Work and sleep. They were one day from taking the flight to Montreal. And that was when Patrick arrived at the rink to watch Scott and Laura work.

They were rehearsing the free dance in their new costumes—mostly black with shiny gold trimming around the neck and wrists, cut to look like funky street clothes, complete with hoods. Laura's hair was tied back in a high, spiky ponytail.

Quietly, Patrick came up and stood next to Vera. Helen Lee joined them from the changing rooms.

"Hi, Patrick. Fasten your seat belt and watch this!" Laura's mum warned.

From the ice, Laura spotted Patrick's arrival. She felt sad for him on his crutches, still looking pale and a bit thinner than before. She waved and gave him a thumbs-up sign.

Then, of course, the moment the first beat of the music played, she forgot everything except the ice. She counted the beat, snaked her hips, and started.

The step sequences went perfectly in this, their last practice before they flew to Canada. They'd speeded up everything to keep perfect time. Vera had added a last-minute degree of difficulty here and put in an extra spin there. *Yes!* Laura said to herself during the dance-off section. *This is beginning to feel like fun!* Even the big, difficult lift went perfectly.

Exhilarated, she and Scott struck their final pose, down on both knees, arms folded, staring at their audience.

Then Laura sprang up and skated quickly toward Patrick. *Please say you liked it!* she thought.

Patrick gave a small shake of his head.

"What's wrong—are you in shock?"

Laura tried to make a joke. *Oh God, he doesn't like it. He thinks we're crazy!*

Her old partner stared at her new partner, who had just skated alongside her, still out of breath, but with a grin across his face. "Hey, Patrick!" Scott said brightly, but he was met by a stunned silence.

It was Vera who stepped in and broke it. "Free dance!" she explained. "Something a little different."

"A *little* different!" Laura grinned awkwardly, desperate for Patrick to approve, yet knowing how hard this must be for him. "Scott looks so cool, doesn't he? He's worked so hard and done so well!"

The small frown that was creasing Patrick's brow slowly faded. "Not exactly what I expected," he muttered, shaking his head again. "I've only ever seen stuff like that on MTV."

"But?" Laura prompted. If Patrick approved, she could step onto that plane with a spring in her step. She could dance in Montreal with a clear conscience.

"But amazing!" Patrick told her. He shook his head over and over again, lost for words. "I don't believe it, it's so . . ."

". . . cool?" Laura suggested.

Patrick nodded. "Cool! New . . . exciting . . . stunning . . . unbelievable!"

"Thanks for saying that, Patrick—I'm so happy!" Laura exclaimed, giving him a first-time-ever hug.

"Yeah, well, just win that medal," he told her, squirming with embarrassment. "Don't come back with a bronze or silver. Remember, only the gold will do!"

Chapter 10

Abi and Georgina and the kids at school would never believe it, Laura thought, looking back on the day of the flight to Canada.

Here she was in her hotel bed, trying to get some sleep.

They'd never believe I've flown across the Atlantic without even looking out the window or watching a movie on my own personal screen. They'll say I'm seriously dumb not to have noticed the mountains or to have gotten the autographs of the famous ice dancers we met on the bus from the airport to the hotel!

It had all happened in such a whirl—the saying good-bye to Immy, Jimmy, Jack, and her mum and dad at the airport, boarding the plane, even the flying, with Vera on one side and Scott in the window seat, going on about the mountains and rivers that he could see way below.

And then they had landed and gone through immigration, clutching their hand luggage containing their skating costumes. Then there was the baggage claim, crowded with other skaters from their competition, arriving from Eastern Europe and the United States. Vera had run into old friends and colleagues and talked nonstop on the bus, while both Scott and Laura were in a daze.

"Sleep!" Vera had instructed them both as soon as they'd had dinner at the hotel. "You must be ready mentally and physically for the compulsory dance tomorrow morning."

No time to think, no time to get nervous. Just sleep.

"Please let it go well tomorrow!" Laura murmured into the darkness. It didn't feel like bedtime. Her body clock was all wrong. "Please let us not make any stupid mistakes. Let everything be as good as it can possibly be!"

"Is it always as bad as this?" Scott asked Laura as they watched the American junior champions come off the ice after their compulsory program.

Laura nodded. "The waiting's the worst part." She and Scott had to skate second to last, hanging around until almost all of the other pairs had performed.

"I don't know how you stand it," he muttered. "My nerves are shot!"

"Ssh!" Laura wanted to concentrate on the American score—18.25 for technical merit, 18.63 for program components. That put them in second place behind the Italians. The American couple hugged their coach and then sat down to watch the next pair.

"Really, I mean it—this is killing me!" Scott whispered. His throat felt dry, and his palms were sweaty. "It's worse than any soccer final!"

Laura managed a grin. "Remember to tell Will that!" she said. Now it was the Russians' turn, who were dressed in scarlet from head to toe. They danced confidently, with perfectly matched leg lines and a seriously good curve lift.

"Too close to the boards on the serpentine steps," Vera muttered, ever critical.

There was a long wait for the scores—18.49 and 19.07 —a total of 37.56, pushing them ahead of the Americans but still behind the Italians at 38.20.

"How long now?" Scott groaned. The idea of being out on the ice in front of the huge crowd, with the judges watching every move, scared the life out of him. "I want to get this over with and then curl up and die!"

"Tttutt!" Vera clicked her tongue, telling Scott to lift up his skates so that she could check his blades. "You can do this. Keep your focus. Don't let the nerves get to you."

I hope he can do it! Laura thought to

herself. *Don't let us down, Scott!*

They watched two more couples dance before their own names were announced.

"Laura Lee and Scott Yorke for the United Kingdom!"

Laura felt the sudden thrill of her name being called. She took a deep breath, glanced at her partner, and then skated smoothly out onto the ice.

This is it—paso doble! Think proud, think Latin—arch your back, lift your head, look like a Spanish princess!

Scott took up his position, and the music began. He let it guide his movements, transforming his laid-back posture into a fiery Latin, foot-stamping stance.

Okay, good! Laura knew that she and Scott were exactly on the beat. She felt the strong overhead lights beat down on them, highlighting every step.

Halfway through, and it was going well. Her silver chiffon skirt fluttered around her legs as Scott made the first lift, and she soared through the air like a shiny bird.

Cool! Now, stay away from the boards, pick up more speed, watch the right foot on the twizzle—not quite perfect—get back together for the three inside turns—better! Okay, now spin and strike a pose!

Before they knew it, the program was over. The audience clapped. Someone in the crowd waved a giant U.K. flag.

"Pretty good," Vera told them as they rejoined her and sat down for the anxious wait for their score.

18.36 and 18.92!

"Third place!" Vera said.

Scott clenched his fists. Laura held her breath. Third after the compulsory section, behind Italy and Russia! As the final couple skated and failed to challenge the leaders, Laura bit her lip and shook her head.

"Cool!" she whispered. "We're in with a real chance of a medal!"

It was weird what happened when you

were on an adrenaline high. First, you could feel your heart racing. Second, you talked too fast and couldn't stop.

"Slow down!" Vera ordered Laura, dragging her away from the rink, where the big Zamboni machine was sweeping around, resurfacing the ice. The coach took Laura and Scott out for lunch. "You need to stay calm and save your strength for the original dance this afternoon."

The restaurant was crowded with competitors from around the world, many of whom had met before. They spoke English, discussing the morning's performances, and all were eager to meet Laura's new partner.

"Where did you find him?" Nina Simakova asked Laura enviously. "He's too good!"

Scott blushed and continued eating.

"I know." Laura smiled back. "I found him at our local rink, actually!"

And the Russian girl grinned and walked

away, thinking that Laura had been kidding.

"Hey, I heard about Patrick's accident." Michelle Lamoureux came up next to give Scott the third degree. "Where did you learn to skate? How come the Brits have been hiding you away until now?"

"I learned at my local rink," he insisted. "Laura kind of forced me into this."

The Canadian girl laughed. "No way!"

"I'm serious."

"Wow!" Realizing that he was, Michelle went off to tell the others.

Scott frowned and looked at Laura. "What am I—some kind of freak?"

It was her turn to laugh. She thought of how far he'd come—and how fast. "Nope, you're a skating superstar!" she told him. "But don't let it go to your head!"

"Okay, now, not too much drama, like with the Italians," Vera warned them before they went out to skate the salsa routine.

We have to hold onto third place! Laura

told herself. *I know we can do it—and maybe even get one better!*

The Italian pair had slipped to second place behind the Russians. The U.S. was pushing the U.K. hard from fourth place.

"Next to skate, Laura Lee and Scott Yorke, in third place for the United Kingdom!"

"Enjoy!" Vera whispered, launching them into their original program.

Yeah, enjoy! Laura smiled at Scott. *How cool is this! Pinch me and tell me I'm not dreaming.*

The bright lights shone down. They were ready to begin.

Keep to the beat, keep a clean line, kick, turn, kick! Think about your balance, stay in time, go into the split, come up, and spin. Laura and Scott attacked their serpentine steps with loads of energy and fun.

Then they slowed for the rumba section, leaning in, winding around each other, going into a smooth, silky lift as the trumpet sounded.

Shaky landing! Laura told herself. She felt her right skate wobble before she righted herself. But would the judges have noticed?

They sprang back into a salsa rhythm, matching their steps and leg lines, covering the ice faster than they ever had before, ending with a low spin for Laura while Scott turned and swung his leg over her head.

They finished and skated toward Vera, whose blank expression gave nothing away.

"Did you see my bad landing?" Laura whispered, hardly daring to look up at the scoreboard.

The coach nodded.

"Hey, chill out," Scott said. "It was one tiny mistake!"

But it was enough to push them into fourth place and out of the medals for now. As the scores appeared, Laura's heart sank. "It was that stupid landing!" she muttered bitterly. "Look what I did—I went and knocked us out of the bronze-medal position!"

Chapter 11

There was nothing to do that night but go to bed and sleep on it.

Vera had done her best to talk Laura out of her bad mood, promising that everything would look different tomorrow. "Fourth place is good," she'd urged. "It means you still have everything to skate for."

"Yeah, look at us." Scott was still amazed by the whole scene. "We're dancing with the best in the world here. I mean, these kids have talent!"

But Laura still went to her room blaming herself for her mistake, and when she spoke to her mum on the phone, she couldn't help letting her disappointment show.

"It wasn't Scott letting me down," she told her. "It was the other way around."

"Listen, I'm sure you're exaggerating," Helen replied. "You're not going to be one hundred percent perfect through all three programs—that's impossible."

"Yeah, but I was careless—it shouldn't have happened." Laura· knew that she shouldn't beat herself up and decided to try to sound more positive. "Anyway, maybe tomorrow we'll get through the whole thing without a mistake."

"That's better!" her mum said. "You know we'll all be thinking about you. Immy says to tell you good luck."

"Sweet!" Laura smiled and then sighed. "Wish you were here, Mum."

"Me, too, honey."

"Okay, I'll skate for you and Dad tomorrow. I'll make you proud."

"Laura, we already are as proud as could be! Now go to sleep. Oh, and tell Scott good luck from us. Tell him we think he's amazing!"

"If you two pull this off, it will be the biggest surprise in ice-dancing history!" Vera gave Scott and Laura their final pep talk. She had taken them to one side just seconds before they were due on the ice. "But, remember, we are taking a big risk, and it might not pay off!"

"It will!" Laura gathered her courage by clenching her fists. The scores had just come up for Nina Simakova and her partner, Anton Kuznetsov. The Russians had pushed themselves into the lead. Now it was all down to Laura and Scott.

"It will be a big shock for the judges, remember." Wanting to prepare Laura, Vera laid it on the line. "We have made sure that all the components are within the rules, but the style is not what they expect."

Laura nodded. "I hear you." For a split second, she felt doubt. Then she shut it out. "Y'know what, Scott?"

"What?" he asked, hearing their names called and turning toward the bright rink.

Laura stepped onto the ice beside him, dressed in her blingy black half shirt and pants. "We're definitely, one hundred percent for sure, going to make ice-dancing history!"

The music began. A gasp went up in the audience.

"Come to the hip-hop jam, come to the jitterbug jam . . . at the hip-hop shop you don't stop . . ." Drums sounded the rhythm, one track cutting into another, the DJ dragging a record back and forth to cut and scratch and break and chop the rhythm.

Scott and Laura leaped into action, jerking their bodies to the broken beat, racing across the ice with a string of funky steps and jumps.

The audience fell silent. Was this serious? What were the British dancers up to?

Laura sensed the confusion. *Hey!* she

said to herself. *If we go down, at least we go down big-time!*

Scott reached out for her hand, and together they went into a series of twizzles before they went back-to-back and linked elbows to go into the level-four lift. Laura rolled off Scott's back and clasped her arms around his neck, flinging her legs backward as he stood up into a spin.

The audience gasped again. Someone clapped. Others joined in over the drumbeats and the scratch-and-cut sounds of the hip-hop music.

And now Laura and Scott were whizzing across the ice, keeping a clean line, going for the highest levels of difficulty on a double throw loop and then a triple.

Perfect so far. Laura's confidence rose. Scott was completely into the music, skating beautifully. He danced like nothing else in the world mattered, as if he was alone on the local rink and was just doing his thing.

And Laura did too, flinging herself into more twists and combination spins, grooving to the sound of the drums that thumped their urgent beat across the arena.

They danced their funky hip-hop dance until the music ended.

There was a second of stunned silence, which seemed to last forever, and then the crowd broke into thunderous applause. People rose to their feet and stamped, lifting their hands over their heads and clapping. British fans waved banners and flags. The whole place jumped with the thrill of what they'd just witnessed.

Laura beamed at the excited crowd. Scott looked at her and laughed. "Wicked!"

Together, they left the ice.

Vera greeted them with a broad smile. "So perfect!" she told them with tears in her eyes. "Laura, Scott—I could not have asked for more!"

Her coach's praise and tears meant everything to Laura. She flung her arms around her. "Thank you for believing in us!" she said.

Scott, too, was choked with emotion. "Man, that was the best time!" he said and sighed.

But now they had to wait for the judges. While the crowd kept up their cheers and chants, Laura, Scott, and Vera raised their eyes to the scoreboard.

The scores came up on the electronic board. None of the judges had given a minus score. Three of the nine gave +2 for technical merit, and two had awarded top scores for interpretation.

Laura saw the figures dance and blur in front of her eyes. Her mind refused to do the math. Had they pulled ahead of the Americans, the Russians, and the Italians? Had they won the gold medal?

There was a roar from the crowd. Everyone went wild. The other competitors ran up to congratulate them.

"What did we win?" Laura gasped.

"Gold!" Scott said, raising her hand into the air. "We did it, Laura. We won the gold medal!"

For days, Laura's feet didn't touch the ground and the smile didn't leave her lips.

There were congratulations and parties, interviews with the press, and more parties. Laura and Scott's performance made it onto the sports pages of the Canadian newspapers. *Hip-Hopping into the Future of Ice Dancing! New Kids on the Block Snatch Gold!*

Then they were on the plane home, flying out of Montreal and back to reality. Back to Immy, waiting with Laura's dad at the airport, and big hugs from her kid sister, who insisted on wearing Laura's shiny gold medal around her neck as they drove home.

And home, where the parties started all

over again with family and friends, where questions rained down on Scott and Laura's heads: "How did it feel to win gold?" "Were you a bag of nerves?" "Was the hard work worth it?"

In the end, Laura was sick of being a celebrity. All she longed to do was get back on the ice and skate.

"I'm up to here with partying!" she told Scott after their local newspaper had come to the rink to take pictures of them holding up their gold medals and grinning at the camera. "Give me twizzles and death spirals any day!"

He laughed. "I always said that you were crazy."

"You mean you're not dying to learn another routine with me?" Laura asked with a grin. She knew full well what Scott's answer would be.

In the distance, Scott's friends were hanging out at the entrance, dressed in their United uniforms and carrying sports bags. They were waiting for Scott to join them for a coaching session at the main training ground.

He made shock-horror gestures and backed away. "No, please, no more Scary Woman forcing my body into unnatural positions and making me ache from head to toe! No more early mornings, no more bling!"

It was Laura's turn to laugh. "Wimp! But—admit it—you had fun!"

Scott looked her in the eye. "Okay, I did. And you know what?"

"What?"

"You're really something, Laura Lee. One in a million, if you ask me."

"You, too, Scott Yorke," she managed to say. Then there were blushes all around. *Oops, this is getting too serious—let me out of here!* Laura thought of being back on the ice with Vera, training for the next competition, when Patrick's leg would have healed and the old partnership would be back in action.

Soon Scott was on his way, hands in his pockets, new sunglasses hiding his eyes, to meet his friends.

And Laura was on the ice. She was lost in her own world of double lutzes, triple loops, and double twists.

Want to read more exciting sports stories?
Here's the first chapter from Donna King's
Game, Set, and Match*!*

"You're a winner, Leo, and you have big dreams."

Carrie Springsteen read her horoscope and sighed.

"You get right where the action is, and don't you just love it when the spotlight is on you!"

No! Carrie thought. *Okay, so I have big dreams of winning in tennis, but that spotlight stuff—no way!*

She sat cross-legged on the grassy slope, reading her magazine. Although she had an August birthday, she didn't see herself as a typical Leo show-off. More of a shy type, really.

"Good shot, Joey!" Hilary called across the net to the dark-haired kid she was coaching on a nearby court.

Carrie glanced up, sighed again, and then closed her magazine. Joey's session was about to end. *Me next,* she thought.

Her dad came down the steps from the clubhouse. "Hey, Carrie, why aren't you warming up? Come on, pick up your racket—the summer vacation may have begun, but we can't have you slouching around."

So she sprang onto her feet, and they headed to the practice court. For ten minutes Carrie hit a ball against the concrete wall.

"Nice work!" her dad told her. "That backhand is really improving. Most grown-ups can't hit the ball that hard. Good job!"

Carrie grinned at him. She felt good— ready to start work with Hilary.

"Hi, Carrie!" The coach greeted her with a wide smile. "How's my star player?"

"Great, thanks." Carrie took up her position across the net from Hilary. She checked her grip and waited for the first ball.

Whack! She hit it in the middle of the strings and returned it fast and low.

"Good shot!" Hilary called.

She nodded and smiled. *Yeah, that felt cool!* Carrie pushed a stray strand of fair hair back from her face and tucked it into her ponytail.

"Again!" Hilary instructed.

Whack! Carrie played the same shot. It zoomed across the net.

"Watch your position. Move your feet!" her dad shouted from the sideline.

Carrie nodded. She crouched and waited. The next ball came toward her, and she hit it hard.

"Nice one!" Hilary said, studying Carrie's backhand.

They'd been playing for almost an hour without a break. Carrie's dad made sure that there was no "slouching around," as he called it.

"Move your feet!" he had yelled over and over. "Come on, Carrie! Run!"

It was hot. She was tired. The palm of her racket hand was sticky with sweat.

"We've got the County Championship coming up this weekend," Martin Springsteen reminded Hilary. "Carrie needs to be at the top of her game."

"She's playing really well," the coach told him. "Her backhand drive is her strongest shot. For a twelve-year-old player, it's the best I've seen."

"Yeah, but she still has to work on the rest of her game." Carrie's dad wanted his golden girl to win. He was determined to make her the best. Ever since Carrie had been able to hold a tennis racket, he'd had his heart set on producing a Grand Slam champion.

Hilary glanced up at the hot sun. "Let's take a break," she suggested.

"No, we haven't had our full hour," Martin argued, checking his watch. "Keep playing, Carrie. You need to practice your serve."

★ ★ ★

The hour of coaching was over at last. Carrie was in the changing room, getting ready to take a shower. She unlaced her tennis shoes and threw them under the bench. Then she unzipped her dress and loosened her long hair. Turning on the shower, she tilted her head back and let the cool spray sprinkle her cheeks.

Good shot! . . . Nice serve! . . . Game, set, and match to Carrie Springsteen! For her whole life she'd been hearing that stuff.

Carrie's a natural tennis player . . . She has buckets of talent . . . That girl will go far!

At five years old Carrie had been spotted by the coach at the fancy club where her mum and dad played tennis. At seven she'd been put into a special program for talented tennis kids.

"Carrie's the one to watch," everyone said. "She's a future Grand Slam champion. She's a star!"

Under the shower Carrie could hear all

those voices inside her head.

Okay, at 12 she could hit the ball harder than most adults. She had the longest legs, terrific speed, and lightning-quick reactions. She *was* good!

But lately she didn't go out on the court with a spring in her step like she had last year and all the years before. Carrie took a sharp breath. Maybe she was tennised out!

Take last night, when her best friend, Liv, had called.

"I'm meeting Alice and Mandi in town tomorrow at ten. We're going shopping. Can you come?" she asked.

"Sorry, I can't," Carrie said.

"Okay, don't tell me. You're playing TENNIS." Liv had said the word in capital letters—like, TENNIS MENACE!

"Yeah." Carrie's voice was flat. She was missing out again.

It was the story of her life. Tennis triumph and social life sadness.

Sorry I can't come to the dance/party/ movies . . . I need an early night . . . I'm playing in a tournament. For Carrie, tennis always had to come first.

Sighing, she turned off the shower and got dressed. *Ouch!* She felt a small pain in her thigh, as if she'd pulled a muscle. Pressing her thumbs into the spot, she massaged the ache.

"Hey, Carrie, are you limping?" Hilary asked as she came out of the changing room and onto the balcony overlooking the courts. The coach had been talking with Martin Springsteen while he waited for his daughter to shower and change.

"It's nothing," Carrie answered.

"Are you sure you don't want Hal to take a look?" Hilary asked.

"No, thanks." Hal was the physiotherapist, but Carrie didn't think the pain was serious.

"Probably just a cramp," her dad guessed, taking her sports bag and heading off down the steps toward the car.

For a few seconds Carrie hung back.

"Is everything okay?" Hilary asked. She knew that Carrie was shy and wouldn't always say what she was thinking.

"Yep." Carrie couldn't think of what else to say. Anyway, her dad was waiting.

"Well, good luck in the under-fourteens this Saturday," Hilary said.

Carrie smiled and nodded.

"The County Championship is a good one to win," her coach reminded her. "It'll get you noticed at a national level—the big time!"

Where the action is—the spotlight! Carrie swallowed hard. "Thanks!"

Hilary gazed at Carrie—at her wide, blue eyes and her sunburned face. "You can do it!" she said quietly.

Carrie gave Hilary a final nod before she followed her dad down the steps. The ache in her leg was still there, she noticed.

"Your mum called—lunch is ready," her dad said as she got into the car.

She took out her phone and read her text messages as they drove home.

Gd luck on Sat Alice had texted.

Bought cool shirt Liv wrote.

Cool Carrie texted Liv back. Then she stared out the window while her dad talked tactics for the weekend's matches.

"Plenty of topspin on your second serve . . . good, solid baseline play . . . don't take risks . . . wait for your opponent to make the mistakes . . ."

Yeah, Dad, whatever! she thought. She rubbed the ache on the side of her thigh. *But do you know what? Okay, you and Mum want me to be a tennis star more than anything else in the world. But the way I feel right this minute, I wouldn't care if I never picked up another tennis racket in my whole life!*